Symbols
of faith

faith formation and sacramental preparation
for people with learning disabilities

Diana Klein

in collaboration with

Caritas
St Joseph's

Acknowledgements

These materials were written in collaboration with the team at St Joseph's Pastoral Centre: John Coleby, Sue Day, Gail Williams, Finola Ryan and Sue Pratt.

We acknowledge, with thanks, the significant contribution to this project made by the Jerusalem Trust and to the St John Southworth Fund and Jar Trust for their contributions.

Thanks to Liz O'Brien (Special Needs Adviser, Birmingham Diocese), Cristina Gangemi (Kairos Forum University of Aberdeen) and Sheila Isaac (pastoral assistant and former outreach worker at St Joseph's Pastoral Centre) for their advice and assistance.

Thanks to Daniel O'Leary (a priest of Leeds Diocese) for reviewing and commenting on the materials and to Paul Turner (a priest from Missouri, USA) for reviewing and commenting on the materials, particularly in relation to the adaptation of the rites of the RCIA.

And, special thanks to the people with learning disabilities and their parents/carers for their advice and assistance in writing these materials, especially: Jenny and Siobhan Fairclough, David and Theresa Tunnell. St Joseph's Pastoral Centre is grateful to the National Council of the Churches of Christ in the USA for the use of the New Revised Standard Version Bible: Catholic Edition copyright ©1993 and 1989. All rights reserved.

Widgit Symbols © Widgit Symbols 2002-2014 www.widgit.com.

CARITAS ST JOSEPH'S
working with people with learning disabilities
St Joseph's Pastoral Centre, St Joseph's Grove, The Burroughs, Hendon, London NW4 4TY
Telephone: 020 8202 3999; fax: 020 8202 1418
E-mail: enquiries@stjoseph.org.uk; website: www.stjoseph.org.uk
Registered Charity No. 233699

Table of Contents

Notes about terminology used in these materials:

1. In these materials, we have used the term "learning disabilities". Up to recently, the term "learning difficulties" has also been used. There has been a shift towards using the term "intellectual disabilities" instead, as a broader concept encompassing various intellectual or cognitive deficits, which includes specific learning difficulties or disabilities.

2. We refer to the people being catechised as "participants" or "candidates". Your group may be small or large and we would like to see everyone as a participant in the session.

3. We refer to your time together as "sessions", not "classes". This emphasises that you are meeting together and sharing together; the parents, priests or catechists are catechists, leaders of the sessions, not teachers.

Welcome to *Symbols of Faith*

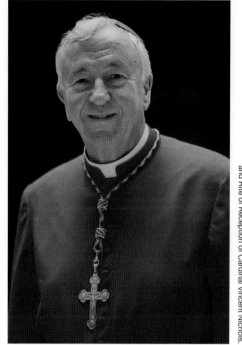

Dear parents, priests and catechists,

"The members of the body that seem to be weaker are indispensable" (1 Corinthians 12:22). This short passage of scripture proclaims a very powerful and important message.

How often do we count ourselves among the weak? Or consider ourselves useless, not needed? It is a huge comfort to be assured by God's Word that we are not! This should make us conscious of those who are deemed weak by society and, indeed, sometimes by us.

Writing this foreword, I am thinking particularly of people with learning disabilities. As St Paul says, "they *seem* to be weaker". Our misperception of those with learning disabilities is revealed as just that, misrepresentation. In contrast, we are asked to recognise their indispensability.

This is why I enthusiastically welcome *Symbols of Faith*. It is rooted in the conviction that our brothers and sisters with learning disabilities are indispensable parts of the One Body. The material that *Symbols of Faith* provides is a great practical tool for those who work, and learn from, the members of our community who seem to be weaker. *Symbols of Faith* both recognises and ensures that those faithful with learning disabilities have a rightful place in the very heart of the Church.

I will keep in my prayers all who use *Symbols of Faith*: the parents, the priests, the catechists and above all the people with learning disabilities.

May God bless you all.

His Eminence Cardinal Vincent Nichols, Archbishop of Westminster
January 2015

Introduction for parents, priests and catechists

*"I never knew what love was until I was loved by someone
who could do nothing for me but love me."*

The rationale for these materials is to provide resources for those engaged in faith formation and sacramental preparation within the context of people with learning disabilities. These materials are part of a twofold package:

- This book for parents, priests and catechists offers guidance in leading people with learning disabilities through the process of learning more about their faith, and preparing them to celebrate the sacraments.
- There is a CD of additional resources in the back cover of this book, which provides you with ready-made pages to complement the sessions in this book.

Parents have the first responsibility for forming their children in faith; priests must provide formation in the parish and catechists support the parents and priests. This book aims to lead you through the process by providing suggestions for activities to link human experiences with religious experiences and to help people with learning disabilities develop their awareness of God's presence in their lives.

The materials aim to help you help people with learning disabilities reach their fullest capacities as human beings by learning more about themselves and celebrating their lives. Consideration has been given to providing activities and experiences that will be motivating, enjoyable and accessible across the different levels. They are on CD so that you can personalise the human and religious experiences to suit the ability of your candidate(s).

An important discovery that has emerged in recent years is the policy of greater inclusion and diversity. This has led to our recognition of the wide variety of ways of breaking open the Good News for people who communicate differently. In the context of faith, it demands the fine tuning of all our faculties, not just our reason, and has the benefit of taking us to the heart of scripture and faith.

Pope Benedict XVI began his first encyclical, *Deus Caritas Est*, with these words from the first Letter of John: "God is love, and he who abides in love abides in God, and God abides in him." (1 John 4:16)

I have written these materials so that they can be used in the most flexible way possible. They are for baptised people and people who might want to be baptised. Baptised Catholic people may be preparing for confirmation or for their First Holy Communion; or this may be an opportunity of faith formation they have not had before. People who are baptised in another Christian denomination may be asking to become Catholic. Their formation will lead to being received into full communion with the Catholic Church (when they will be confirmed and receive the Eucharist). Unbaptised people may be preparing for baptism, confirmation and the Eucharist (in keeping with the Rite of Christian Initiation of Adults, the RCIA).

The most important thing to remember in any Christian faith formation is to help us to know Jesus, or to know him more deeply. He is the one who reveals the love of the Father in the Spirit. Christians are followers of Jesus; and, as his followers, we aim to be more and more like him.

People with learning disabilities do not lack in their ability to love. Many years ago, the mother of a child with learning disabilities summed up what I am trying to say. She said: "I never knew what love was until I was loved by someone who could do nothing for me but love me."

I hope you will find these materials helpful and that you, too, will grow in your love of God.

Diana Klein
January 2015

Teresa and David Tunnell

Understanding these materials

These materials have been designed for use with candidates who respond readily to a sensory approach which uses ritual and symbol to help them connect to their own personal lived experience with the spiritual.

Catechising anyone is a privilege. People are sometimes anxious to make sure that people with learning disabilities understand enough, that they know enough before they can celebrate the sacraments. In fact, the aim of catechesis is to help people come to know Jesus, or to know him more deeply. Any catechist will tell you that it is difficult to know just how successful they have been in helping people to do this, and just how successful they have been when they mediate the Good News of the Gospel. People are tempted sometimes to think that we are doing something special for people with learning disabilities, but are then surprised when they realise that those with learning disabilities have enriched us far more than we have enriched them.

A story comes to mind. There was a priest who went to a new parish and he noticed that every Sunday, a teenage boy with Down's syndrome came for a blessing when his mother came to receive Holy Communion. The priest asked the mother why her son was not

Annual Mass, Westminster Cathedral for people with learning disabilities

photo © St. Joseph's Pastoral Centre

receiving communion. She explained that she had been told that the boy was not capable of understanding sufficiently to receive Holy Communion. The new priest tried to prepare the boy, but he wasn't sure he was getting anywhere. He decided that the boy would receive his First Holy Communion on a particular Sunday. The priest invited the boy and his mother to receive Communion first. With all eyes on them, the boy took the host, he broke it and he gave half to his mother and they consumed it together. Now, ask yourself just what you think that boy understood.

The Church tells us that, given our growth in the understanding of disabilities and the progress we have made in specialised teaching, it is possible and desirable for all to have adequate catechesis. In fact our efforts to find ways of catechising people with learning disabilities, have led to a wide development of alternative and more creative methods of catechesis for all, which do not rely solely on the literate or verbal.

We must meet people where they are, and we must communicate with them in a way they can understand. Another story comes to mind. It is a story that helps people think about how good they are about meeting people where they are.

"Once upon a time a monkey and a fish were in a huge flood. The agile monkey was able to save itself by grasping a tree branch and pulling itself to safety. Happy at last, the monkey noticed a fish fighting against the massive current and, deeply moved by its plight, he bent down to save it. The fish was not happy, for it bit the monkey's hand. Whereupon the monkey, being terribly annoyed at the fish's ingratitude, threw the fish back into the water." [1]

Educational advisers remind parents, teachers and catechists that it is normal to see things from our own point of view, based on our life experience, our abilities, our level of understanding, and so on. In spiritual terms, we talk about this as contextual theology, being able to meet people in the context in which they exist. We must avoid the tendency to be like the bungling monkey in this story!

> "It is possible and desirable for all to have adequate catechesis."
>
> General Directory for Catechesis (GDC 189)

---

[1] D. Adams, 'The Monkey and the Fish: Cultural Pitfalls of an Educational Adviser' in *International Development Review*, vol. 2, no. 2 (1960), pp. 22-24 – as quoted in Arbuckle, *Earthing the Gospel, An Inculturation Handbook for the Pastoral Worker*, Orbis Books, Maryknoll, New York, 1990, p. 1.

Canon Law tells us

According to Canon Law, there is a genuine equality of dignity and action among all of Christ's faithful and, because of their equality, they all contribute – each according to his/her own condition and office, to the building up of the Body of Christ (Code of Canon Law 208).

In 1988, the bishops of England and Wales produced a pastoral document, *Valuing Difference*, which provides practical advice for promoting access and inclusion in all our Church activities to help us build up the Body of Christ through the participation of all its members. In this report, the bishops reminded us that each of us is created in God's image, that God loves us as we are, with our own particular gifts and limitations, strengths and weaknesses and that Christ's liberating message of love and hope celebrates difference because he values each and every person as unique and equal. The bishops also reminded us that Christ teaches us that, through knowing and loving him, each of us can grow in the knowledge and love of God. We are all called to express God's love in our daily life, valuing the difference and equal dignity of every person. Each of us has a unique vocation and mission, and rich diversity of the body of Christ includes those who live with disabilities. The bishops told us that our task, as members of the Church, is to translate Christ's message of inclusion into practical action, so that the contribution of each member is respected and nurtured. They told us that this is our shared mission. For just as each of us receives the gift of the Holy Spirit through baptism, so we can grow as a Church through the gifts each of us brings to the Body of Christ. They said "active participation needs to be accessible to all". (*Valuing Difference*, a report of the Bishops' Conference of England and Wales for People with Disabilities in the life and mission of the Church, 1988, p. 3.)

For those who work in this area of catechesis, the need to explore different ways of experiencing and understanding means that methodologies, approaches and resources have been developed to respond to this need. Our

photo © Diana Klein

"We are the Body of Christ."
1 Corinthians 12:27

10

brothers and sisters in Christ with learning disabilities lead us to ways of doing catechesis and religious education from which the whole community can benefit. It draws us into the very heart and essence of our faith.

Authentic belonging and companionship

It is vital that people with learning disabilities feel that they really belong in our parish communities. Opportunities to mix with other, non-disabled people locally are few and children with learning disabilities may attend a special school away from their home area.

Adults who have learning disabilities may be living away from home. Their staff are not necessarily Christians and are often curtailed in taking people to church through lack of numbers. Companionship with other people who are Catholic is not only about enabling people to go out and to be present at events.

Stable, long-standing friendships help us to learn trust, love for others and enjoyment of creation and life given by God. A faith community is one way of enabling people with and without learning disabilities to share friendship and to experience the presence of God in their midst.

Circles of support

Most people have allies. If things go wrong, allies will be sympathetic, concerned, and interested. They will listen, help out, and seek help from others. If things are going well they will be interested, pleased, and will share the good experience. Crucially, allies do what they do for personal, not professional reasons.

Allies are people who like you and who want to know you, not people who are assigned to your care. For some people it can be helpful when allies meet to listen, share ideas, solve problems, and to plan how to help. If there are particular, identifiable people who show a personal commitment in organising around someone who needs help, it can be helpful to refer to this being the person's circle of support or circle of friends.

A circle of support is what happens when someone's allies get together to co-ordinate their efforts to help. It's not a formal structure, and when we talk about circles of support

Observe good practice in established models where this work is happening effectively. The aim of this guidance is also to lead the Catholic community to the discovery of what is meant in *Valuing Difference* by the statement "part of the body of Christ is missing when any individual is excluded from Church life" *Valuing Difference*, Part 2, p. 9 and by St Paul when he reminds us that "the members of the body that seem to be weaker are indispensable".

1 Corinthians 12.22

we shouldn't forget this. Few people have a clearly defined group of allies. We might have one or two people to whom we are very close, a small group who are key allies, a larger group who are distant friends, and lots of people who have a professional relationship with us but who are also friendly. If we needed some support over an issue in our life some of these people would be willing to organise around us to help out. Allies might gather around us in different ways and at different times. Some would help consistently, and others would help sporadically. Some would always be supportive, and some might be allies at one time and not at another.

For some people it can be helpful when allies meet to listen, share ideas, solve problems, and to plan how to help. If there are particular, identifiable people who show a personal commitment in organising around someone who needs help, it can be helpful to refer to this as being the person's circle of support or circle of friends.

We have drawn on the work of Robert Weetman, *Capacity Thinking Consultancy and Training*, to explain the concept of circles of support. (See www. capacitythinking.org.uk/circles.html for more information).

A circle of support organises around the person at the centre of the circle; the focus person. The people in the circle do the things that come naturally to true allies. They listen; not in the way that people do when consulting, but in the way that friends do. They solve problems by thinking together, bouncing ideas around, checking things out, and by going back to the drawing board over and over again. They pull in favours, put themselves out, and use their contacts. Sometimes they act together, and sometimes each person works alone. They celebrate success together, and they find the failure of their friends disappointing.

© The Tunnell family

David Tunnell surrounded by his circle of support

Circle of intimacy

The diagram to the right shows where you are in the circle. This innermost circle will also include the people closest to you; family members and/or some of your oldest and dearest friends; the people you can't imagine not being around even if you don't see them all that often.

Circle of friendship

The second circle includes the people we think of as friends in the real sense of the word. People we confide in, rely on, borrow money from, laugh and cry with; people who almost made the first circle.

Circle of participation

The third circle includes all the people we meet on a daily basis: people who work in our office, school friends, people who we meet at church or when following our hobbies or interests; people who always say "hello" even though we don't know their first name.

Circle of exchange

This outer circle includes all the people who are *paid* to be in our lives. This might include our doctor, dentist, child-minder, hairdresser, plumber. Most paid support workers will fit in this circle too.

What does your circle look like?

The life of an active adult can include hundreds of relationships. Try filling your circles in. People with learning disabilities, on the other hand, may be limited to family and paid service providers who contribute to their well-being, as shown in these circles of support. Think about how limited the person with learning disabilities is when they are at the centre in terms of "friendships of choice".

Their circle of intimacy

might only include their immediate family.

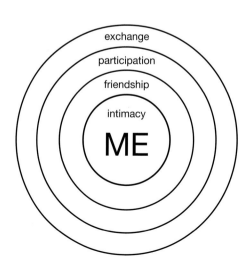

Their circle of friendship

might only include two or three people with whom they are in regular contact, perhaps wherever they live or go for their activities.

Their circle of participation

will include the people they meet at their day centre or at the gym. It might include the priest they meet when they come to church and, perhaps, one of the parishioners they see when they are there.

Their circle of exchange

will include the people who are *paid* to be in their lives. This will include their doctor, dentist, child-minder, hairdresser, plumber, the postman, the local policeman, a shopkeeper and other support workers.

S/he associates with those s/he comes into contact with at the day centre or the sports centre. S/he is supported and served by a social worker, doctors, the postman, and so on and in all likelihood, s/he is identified by them as a person with learning disabilities.

Why these circles are important

The ideas around circles of support become particularly important when we remember that some people:

- have few allies;
- are disempowered by organisations and people who have power over them, limiting their hopes, ambitions and confidence.
- may not be able to tell us about their hopes, dreams and nightmares.

Identity and gifts

Ask yourself how you introduce yourself. You might mention things such as your job, where you're from, where you live, some of your interests. It's useful in a circle of support to take an interest in this same information by asking how the 'focus' person is seen, what kind of hobbies and interests they have, what things are they passionate about and what skills and resources they have. Finding out what they know, and about these other things begins to build a fuller picture of a person. When we talk about "person-centred"

"Every single person has capacities, abilities and gifts. Living a good life depends on whether those capacities can be used, abilities expressed and gifts given. If they are, the person will be valued, feel powerful and well-connected to the people around them; and the community around the person will be more powerful because of the contribution the person is making."

A Guide to Capacity Inventories: Mobilising the Community Skills of Local Residents, John P Kretzmann and John L McKnight, ACTA Publications, Chicago, 1997, p.3

planning in our work with people with learning disabilities, we also talk about the "gifts" people have. In this context, we do not mean someone's ability as a pianist or painter. Rather a gift is a "unique attribute": something about you which creates a possible hook or connection with at least one other person. For example, someone might have a welcoming smile or an ability to be calm and quiet; they may be kind or see themselves as being able to be a good friend. Discovering a person's gifts requires empathy, insight and the simple act of spending time with them.

If you have understood how these circles work, you will be asking:

- How can I help someone bring their allies together?
- How can I make sure that the allies stay motivated when things get difficult?
- How can I make sure that allies working together don't become disempowering?

Faith formation in a circle of support

Ideally, faith formation will take place within a circle of support with people of a similar age, who have similar interests. People of the same age who can offer an experience of friendship and companionship, and a sense of belonging to a group of people: a community which has meaning, both for the candidate and for other members of the community.

Being aware of the range of learning disabilities

When we talk about "people with learning disabilities", be aware that there is a full range of disabilities and you will need to personalise these materials to suit the people you meet.

For example, if you have a deaf person in your group, music may not help that person much; if you have a blind person, you cannot use art and images. Those examples are simple enough to understand; but you might have a speech impaired person, who cannot speak.

MENCAP defines learning disability as a reduced intellectual ability and difficulty with everyday activities; for example household tasks, socialising or managing money, which affects someone for their whole life.

People with a learning disability tend to take longer to learn and may need support to develop new skills, understand complex information and interact with other people. The level of support someone needs depends on individual factors, including the severity of their

Hearing a few key stories, or even a few minor stories, can be revealing and involving. The idea is to get to know the focus person well. Sometimes knowing about someone's history can help a circle to avoid the repetition of past mistakes, or missed opportunities, or lost relationships that can be picked up.

(www.capacitythinking.org.uk/circles.html)

Note: music is not necessarily out of the question with deaf and hearing impaired as many can and do derive pleasure from aspects of music through the rhythm and vibrations they feel and certain sounds they can respond to.
To find out more about learning disabilities: www.mencap.org.uk/all-about-learning-disability.
For more information about ADHD and ADD, see: http://www.nhs.uk/Conditions/Attention-deficit-hyperactivity-disorder/Pages/Introduction.aspx, www.chadd.org, www.add.org www.help4adhd.org.

learning disability. For example, someone with a mild learning disability may only need support with things like getting a job. However, someone with a severe or profound learning disability needs full-time care and support with every aspect of their life; they may also have physical disabilities.

People with certain specific conditions can have a learning disability too. For example, people with Down's syndrome and some people with autism have a learning disability. People who suffer with attention deficit disorder (ADD) will not be able to pay attention for more than a few minutes. ADD is one of the subtypes of attention-deficit hyperactivity disorder (ADHD). ADD is similar to the other subtypes of ADHD in that it is characterised primarily by inattention, being easily distracted, disorganisation, procrastination and forgetfulness. Where it differs from the other subtypes is in lethargy or fatigue, and having fewer or no symptoms of hyperactivity or impulsiveness typical of the other ADHD subtypes.

Learning disability is often confused with dyslexia and mental health problems. Mencap describes dyslexia as a "learning difficulty" because, unlike learning disability, it does not affect intellect. Mental health problems can affect anyone at any time and may be overcome with treatment, which is not true of learning disability. We are discovering that more and more people are dyslexic or suffer with dyspraxia.

Choosing and using resources

The process of selecting and using resources and activities is very important. If people cannot respond well to speaking and listening, or to pictures and storytelling unsupported by the use of other media, you have to find materials that will gain their attention and interest.

photo © The Tunnell family

Once people are engaged, relaxed and happy, it becomes more possible to introduce a theme and mediate a message related to the aim of the session. These materials offer a variety of activities to help you find the best way to do this. If you follow the suggestion in a session to use finger puppets, for example, and you find this an effective way for people to engage with a scripture story, consider making them a frequent part of mediating scripture. Having said that, it would be a pity to use them exclusively, thus depriving people of experiencing other ways to hear the scriptures which they may also find engaging.

In the **mediated learning experience model**, the mediator selects the appropriate materials for the individuals with whom they are working.

Have ready a collection of items and materials which, in relation to the range of people in your group, have the potential to:

- interest, motivate and engage the person with autism and/or severe and complex learning disabilities;
- arouse pleasure, joy, security and calm for the person;
- elicit surprise, curiosity and wonder in the person;
- provide opportunities to relax and calm the more frenetic, hyperactive people;
- help to gradually expand the range of materials the person is willing and able to give attention to;
- provide opportunities for the person to discover and reveal likes and dislikes, preferences and intolerances;
- provide opportunities for structuring peer-awareness, interpersonal tolerance and turn-taking activities.

Your resources must have the potential to elicit surprise, curiosity and wonder.

David Tunnell at the Inclusion Project at Oakwood with St Francis

photo © The Tunnell family

Every item and material you choose must have the potential to form a link or bridge to exploring a theme, or mediating a message, relating to the stated aims and areas of learning you have identified. Your resourcing skills and style will evolve alongside your knowledge and experience of the needs of a wide range of people with autism and learning disabilities.

Alternative ways to communicate

British Sign Language (BSL) is the sign language used in the United Kingdom — and it is the first or preferred sign language here.

Widgit produces a wide range of symbol-supported learning materials and symbol stories, including extensive topic-based packs "ready to go" for special and mainstream education, developed by the Symbol Inclusion Project. To find out more about the Symbols Inclusion Project, visit: www.symbolsinclusion project.org.

Whereas a photograph gives a lot of information, an illustration is simpler and representative of a single idea — but still has some detail. Symbols and icons are all around us, from instructions on an appliance to signs in foreign airports. They give us immediate information which may otherwise be too difficult or time-consuming to access. A road sign in text, for example, would be useless for someone who could not read the language and too time-consuming to be safe for someone who could.

Fr Paul Fletcher (a deaf priest) and Fr Cyril Axelrod (a deaf/blind priest)

Symbols are similar to icons, but are able to convey a much broader and more varied level of meaning. Icons are a visual key used to access a single piece of information and work in isolation from one another. They may have a design which can convey a layered meaning. For example, a road sign within a red triangle is a warning and a red circle with a line through is a prohibition, but they cannot be used to convey anything more than basic information.

Makaton is a language that provides a means of communication to individuals who cannot communicate efficiently by speaking. Almost everything we do involves communication; everyday tasks such as learning at school, asking for food and drink, sorting out problems, making friends and having fun. Makaton has been effectively used with individuals who have cognitive impairments, autism, Down's syndrome, specific language impairment, multi-sensory impairment and acquired neurological task organisation. Deaf blind people learn to communicate using signs, symbols and speech.

TEACCH (Treatment and Education of Autistic and related Communication Handicapped Children): Working from the premise that people with autism are predominantly visual learners, TEACCH's intervention strategies are based around physical and visual structure, schedules, work systems and address difficulties with communication, organisation, generalisation, concepts, sensory processing, change and relating to others. These materials have as a philosophical premise the need for understanding, empathy and sensitivity in relation to the condition or 'culture' of autism. It uses structure and visual clarification to reduce anxiety, and provides predictability and reassurance for people, thus bringing order out of chaos in their experience of the world. Be sure to adapt the materials to suit people with autism.

Symbolism such as Christian artefacts: crucifixes, candles, chalices, patens, rosaries, statues, many of which are easily found in our homes or parishes.

Find out more about Widgit and its symbols support reading texts on www.widgit.com/symbols/about_symbols/index.htm. BSL sign language: www.britishsignlanguage.com. Makaton: www.makaton.org. TEACCH: www.teacch.com. Asperger Syndrome: www.sense.org.uk.
Some people use assistive communication devices and, where possible, it would be beneficial to get information from speech and language therapists/teachers/parents regarding the optimum communication mode for that person so that you can use it. See www.uk.dynavoxtech.com.

The way we grow in faith

The Church tells us there are four ways we grow in faith. They involve the whole person: body, mind, heart and spirit (RCIA 75.1-4).

Note:

The RCIA is the Rite of Christian Initiation of Adults. It is how adults (from age 14 upwards) and children (between 7-14) become Christians today in the Catholic Church. The Church teaches that this is the model for all catechesis.

The first way is by gaining suitable knowledge

The Church tells us that a fitting formation accommodated to the liturgical year and enriched by celebrations of the Word leads us to a suitable knowledge of dogma and an intimate understanding of the mystery of salvation (RCIA 75.1). The key words here are fitting, suitable, intimate. Intimacy happens because the right word is said at the right time in the right way; but all these key words speak of personal knowledge, heart knowledge, something that becomes a part of me. Dogma is the language of how the truths of our faith are believed and communicated. For people with learning disabilities, this begins with our invitation and welcome to come and see where we live (cf John 1:38-39).

Secondly, we learn by living as a Christian

Like the disciples, we come to know Jesus by following him. The Church tells us that we learn to pray to God more easily and exercise charity once we become familiar with living the Christian way of life. We are helped by the example and support of sponsors and godparents and the whole community of the faithful (RCIA 74.2). There is a very close connection between what we believe and how we live. The pathway into community life takes place little by little: "See how they love one another" (John 13:35).

Thirdly, we need to listen to God's Word

The Church says that we learn to pray by celebrating liturgies and by being helped on our journey "little by little" (RCIA 75.3). Our task is to know when and how to celebrate liturgy and to pray in such a way that it touches people's hearts. Remember, we pray in order to encounter God: "I am with you always" (Matthew 18:20).

Prayer helps us become more aware of God's presence in our lives.

Fourthly, we respond to that Word

We walk in God's presence living by faith and using our gifts for the service of others.

The Church tells us that we should learn how to spread the Gospel and build the Church by the witness of our lives (RCIA 75.4). We are led through listening to scripture, through our experience of liturgy, prayer and reflection on scripture and tradition, into relationship with God. This is how we discover how to be followers of Jesus; how to live by faith; discerning how we will use our gifts for the service of others. These are the four different ways of achieving the goal of catechesis.

The RCIA process

is a gradual process of coming to know the person of Jesus and living our lives as one of his followers.

- The first stage begins with the invitation to find out about Jesus or to get to know him better. It is called the Enquiry Period.
  Our first step is to say "yes" to that invitation.
- The second stage is to live with; and to live like; the followers of Jesus. It is called the Period of the Catechumenate.
  The second step is a rite of blessing and healing.
- The third stage is a time of prayer and reflection, when we prepare to celebrate the sacraments of initiation (baptism, confirmation and the Eucharist). It is called the Period of Purification and Enlightenment.
  The third step is the celebration of the sacraments of initiation.
- The fourth stage is living as Christians for the rest of our lives.

This is a very brief explanation of the RCIA process. The stages and steps have been adapted from Part II of the RCIA: Rites for Particular Circumstances. They use the adaptation of the rite to unbaptised children of catechetical age; exceptional circumstances in which the process of Christian initiation is not followed in its complete form.

Photo: Diana Klein

If we can see Jesus, we can see the Father

The disciples asked Jesus to show them the Father; and Jesus told them that if they could see him, they could see the Father (John 14:8-11). Our faith is different from other religions. We believe that God wanted so much for us to know him that he sent his Son as a human being to tell us what he is like.

As we help others to grow in faith, we help them discover where and how they can see Jesus too. After Easter, Jesus taught them that although he was no longer with them, they would be able to see him in a new way. As we help others to grow in faith, we help them discover where and how we can see Jesus today .

Recall how the two friends were walking from Jerusalem to Emmaus sharing their deep concerns about how Jesus had been crucified (Luke 24:13-35). Perhaps they were asking whether they would come to the same end if people found out that they were Jesus' followers. Perhaps they were confused; or they were asking just who Jesus really was. As they went their way, they discussed "all that had happened" (v14) over the previous days, and, as might be expected, it was a "lively exchange" (v15). Who should join them but the risen Jesus, who began to "walk along with them" (v15). Jesus asks them what they have been talking about, why they are so downcast, what's been happening.

Noelle and Ella
Lomanto

22

For whatever reason, they were "restrained from recognising him" (v16). He entered into their company by enquiring: "What are you discussing along your way?" (v17). Somewhat distressed and a little impatient at the stranger's ignorance, they wondered where he had been. Surely, everyone in Jerusalem knew "the things that went on there during these last days" (v18). Rather than seizing this obvious opportunity to disclose his identity he enquired: "What things?" (v19).

Notice in Robert Zünd's picture below, how he captures a walking and talking encounter Jesus was having with the disciples; the kind of encounter he loves to experience with us. Notice, too, how they appear to be walking out of darkness and into the light. We see Jesus as the "light of the world". Perhaps the artist was trying to express the journey the disciples were making out of the darkness of misunderstanding and into the light of understanding.

Notice how the disciples are dressed in red and blue: the colours Jesus is often wearing in icons and paintings. Some say that the blue was used to signify his divine nature (heaven) and the red to signify his human nature (earth or blood). In this picture, however, Zünd

Robert Zünd, *Way to Emmaus*, 1877, Swiss painter (Museum of St Gallen)

has dressed Jesus in white, the colour normally used to depict the resurrected Christ. They told him the story as they knew it and their dwindling hope that "he was the one who would set Israel free" (v21). Now, adding confusion to their disappointment, "some women" (v22) of the group were spreading the "astonishing news" (v22) that "he was alive" (v23).

Notice how they tell him their version of the events that had taken place, and Jesus listened to them. He allowed them to tell the story from their perspective and from their point of view. Think for a moment how important it is to do this in catechesis.

Jesus cajoled them for not looking at these recent events within a broader context, and in response to their story and hope, he told them an older story with a larger vision. He began to open the scriptures, to help them to understand what had happened and how it had been foretold by the prophets beginning with Moses. He "interpreted for them every passage of scripture, which referred to him" (v27). He pointed out that the Messiah had to "undergo all this so as to enter into his glory" (v26). Surely now they would recognise him; but they dId not. Have a look at the painting on the left by Lelio Orsi. Once again, the disciples are leaving the dark and going towards the light, seen by the way the light is reflecting on their clothing. Jesus is dressed in white (although it looks like the white garment is being worn over red trousers).

Lelio Orsi, *On the Way to Emmaus*, 1587. Italian artist (National Gallery, London)

They still didn't recognise Jesus, but Luke tells us that their curiosity was aroused and Jesus continued to resist telling them who he was. They "pressed him" (v29) to stay the night in their company and we know that he agreed. There was something about this stranger. They trusted him. They were open to him. We, too, must invite Jesus 'in' so that he can speak to us, so that we can understand.

It was only when Jesus blessed and broke the bread that "their eyes were opened and they recognised him; whereupon he vanished from their sight" (v31). Notice how Michelangelo da Caravaggio has depicted this moment in the story and notice too, that he paints Jesus wearing a red garment with a white shawl.

Jesus' story was added to their story through the dialogue that took place; but it was only when he blessed and broke the bread that they finally recognised him. When he disappeared, some say he disappeared into them. Ask yourself if that is what happens to us when we receive the Eucharist. The pieces of their puzzle fell into place, and they remembered how their hearts had burned within them as he talked "on the road". But, instead of spending time in self-reproach for not seeing sooner, they set out immediately for Jerusalem (a hazardous journey by night) to tell "the Eleven and the rest of the company" (v33). They wanted to tell the others the Good News; they wanted to share it with them. They'd got the message and they responded by wanting to tell the others that what the women had said was, indeed, true. Jesus was risen and they had seen him.

And so, they told the story of what had happened "on the road" and "how they had come to know him in the breaking of the bread" (v35).

Michelangelo da Caravaggio
Supper at Emmaus, c1601, detail, Italian artist (National Gallery, London)

So, what happened?

The disciples welcomed Jesus

- They told him their story (the human dimension)
- Jesus explained as they shared the scriptures (the religious dimension)
- He made as if to go on; and they invited him to stay with them
- They got the message when he broke the bread
- They wanted to rush back to tell the others the Good News

St Joseph's process

does the same thing:

- We welcome people
- There is an activity (based on the human dimension)
- We explain as we share the scriptures (the religious dimension)
- We invite people to hear Jesus speaking to them.
- People get a message
- They celebrate; they want to share the Good News with each other.

And, on the road we come to know Jesus

Let's look at the process in detail:

Step 1: welcome and gathering

To welcome a fellow human being is to welcome Christ.

It is essential that every member of the group is welcomed by name by one of the catechists. Our names are important to us; remember: God calls each of us by name (Isaiah 43:1).

This kind of welcome sets the scene for all that is to follow, it creates a feeling of warmth and helps people feel at home. It engenders an atmosphere in which trust can develop and it implies that the person welcomed is wanted for their uniqueness, their self, for what their "being" adds to ours. When we call people by name, it can help them to believe it when we say that God calls us each by name.

This is the time when we traditionally introduce people to one another (if necessary), the time when we make sure that nobody is alone and neglected. It is our opportunity to draw together people with and without learning disabilities into companionship, where each accompanies and supports the other. They can get to know each other quietly and join together, at least for a while, on their spiritual journey.

Hospitality and welcome are a very deep part of our spiritual roots. In the Acts of the Apostles, we are told of the early Christian community: "The whole group of believers was united heart and soul" (Acts 4:32). St Paul, in his letter to the Church in Rome, exhorted members to "love each other as much as brothers and sisters should, and have a profound respect for each other . . . . If any of the saints are in need, you must share with them; and you should make hospitality your special care" (Rom 12:10-14).

This message of welcome we give at the start is crucial in building up relationships and trust. It is a way of echoing the Good News of Christ Jesus. In our welcome, we show togetherness as part of the community of church. We show that we matter to each other and that we need each other; this is how we show we love each other.

For reflection:

Dorothy Day, in her autobiography, wrote: "We cannot love God unless we love each other. We know him in the breaking of the bread, and we are not alone any more. Heaven is a banquet and life is a banquet too, even with a crust, where there is companionship. We have all known the long loneliness and we have seen that the only solution is love and that love comes with community."

(Dorothy Day, *The Long Loneliness: Autobiography of the Legendary Catholic Social Activist*, Harper Collins, 2009)

The environment

As we support and catechise people, we become more and more aware of the environment in which we meet people with learning disabilities and their friends; their faith community. It must be welcoming and must convey a sense of warmth, calm and beauty.

Sometimes, we are fortunate enough to have a light, airy and attractive room to meet in; but other times we simply have to do our best to make the best of the environment we have. The five senses (sight, smell, taste, touch, hearing) are all brought into play when we enter any environment. It is important to think of each sense as we consider how to improve our environment, to make it harmonise and to help us focus on Jesus, God's Word and the spiritual dimension of the session. Knowing that everything has been prepared carefully enables the catechists to create an atmosphere of calm, where nothing has to be rushed.

If we take into account how the room affects us, we will have a good guide to what is good and what can perhaps be improved. Small things can make all the difference.

Step 2: the human dimension

During this part of the session, we introduce people to the theme of the session. Then, we talk about "what" the human dimension is in this session. For example, in the sessions on Belonging, we can talk about our experience of belonging. What kind of things do we belong to? What kind of things belong to us? The aim of this session is to reflect on the concept of belonging to God. So we ask the question: What is it like to belong to a family? In the photo below right, we see a girl with her dad. She belongs to him; he belongs to her.

It is important to have symbols to express our experience. In the session on belonging, the symbol we suggest you make a name tag. The one we suggest in session 1 includes the scripture passage from Isaiah 43:1. God calls us by name; we are his. By focusing on the idea that our names belong to us, we can be led gently into the concept that God calls us by name and we belong to him.

In this part of the session, participants ask the "why" question. Why is it good to belong to our families, why do we want others to know our name and why do we want to know other's names? You don't have to ask these questions; simply let them arise as part of the conversation.

Note:

Some people may not be able to engage in discussion about what it means to belong or be able to communicate about their belongings. They may be drawn into the theme of belonging through a song/music activity which recognises, celebrates and thanks God for the "belongings" which are special to them. For example: "Thank you, God, for Jenny's daddy x3, Thank you, God, our Father", sung to the tune of "Skip to my Lou".

Beware: questions can be threatening; and yes/no answers can curtail conversation. Remember how Jesus allowed the disciples to tell him their story of what had happened from their perspective. It is not always easy to listen to others describe what has happened in their lives, especially if you don't remember the event in the same way as they do or if you know there are factual inaccuracies. But it is imperative to respect the way they tell their story, to listen to them and to affirm them. Remember: there are no wrong answers!

By using discussion, activities, art and music, we invite people to explore the links. What we are doing is reflecting more deeply on their story, opening it up so that they can make links to the next part of the session.

This part of the session also helps the participants come to a certain "consciousness". We use memory, imagination and reason and the participants are encouraged to examine why they believe the things they believe. This enables the participants to share in dialogue their own stories. Tom Groome calls this part of the process "critical reflection". Note: you can allow other participants to ask questions about the stories they are hearing so long as they do not silence the one telling their story. (Thomas Groome, *Christian Religious Education – Sharing Our Story and Vision*, Harper Collins Publishers, New York, 1980, p. 191.)

Jenny Fairclough and her dad

photo © The Fairclough family

Step 3: the religious dimension

We are now ready to make the transition to the next part of the session, and we move to a different place, which we call a special place. Ideally, this should be a different room; but if that is not possible, it should be in a separate part of the room we are in.

The prayer focus should be beautiful, a place we want to be. There are many examples in scripture telling us that Jesus went to a special place when he wanted to pray. Luke says he often withdrew to a lonely place and prayed (Luke 5:16).

A focal point used by St Joseph's Pastoral Centre. Notice: the open book with the ribbon page mark, the icon of Jesus,the candle, the beautiful cloth and the flowers

Matthew says he went up on a mountainside by himself (Mt 14:23). Mark tells us that very early in the morning, while it was still dark, Jesus got up, left the house and went off to a solitary place, where he prayed (Mk 1:35). We follow his example by going to a special place where we can find Jesus to listen to him and to talk to him. The icon and the holy book remind us Jesus is there.

The special place

Central to the special place are a holy book and a picture or icon of Jesus. They are concrete evidence that Jesus is with us, that we are there with him and we have come to listen to Jesus speaking to us. The scripture chosen for each session is related to the theme of the session. You might play some quiet music and use this time to light the candle, reminding people that this is another symbol of Christ's presence among us and in the world. Take your time in making this transition to the special place by pausing for a time of quiet until you are ready to begin. Our role is to help each other to hear God speaking to us in our lives today, to help us to experience God's love.

Greeting and reading the scripture

If possible, greet the reading from scripture with an appropriate acclamation. One idea that works for Old Testament and New Testament readings (for children) uses the tune of "London Bridge": We have come to hear God's Word, hear God's Word, hear God's Word. We have come to hear God's Word, let us listen! Many other acclamations are suggested in the materials which are suitable. Signing the head, the mouth and the heart is also a good thing to instil our belief that when we hear God's Word, we understand in our minds, proclaim it with our mouths and feel it in our hearts.

When we listen to scripture, we believe that Jesus is speaking to us right now at this present time. We show this by treating the holy book with great reverence. We read the scripture as follows:

- The reader picks up the book and, holding it up high, reads reverently and clearly to the whole group.
- After putting the holy book back in its special place, the reader holds the hands of each person in the group, one-by-one, and tells them the core of the message of the scripture, that is, in the session on Belonging: "[Name] Jesus says to you today: my father has called you by your name; you are his."
- The reader then reads the scripture again making a wide gesture, which includes

The holy book should be beautiful or should be decorated beautifully. In it, we place a simplified or shortened reading. The book should be open to the place where the reading is. The reading should be typed nicely (ideally on similar paper to the pages in the book and in a typeface to match the text in the book) to maintain the beauty and the continuity of the printed word. There should be an icon, crucifix, statue or picture of Jesus and one or more candles with suitable holders and long matches or a taper. Candles come in many shapes, sizes and scents and, if possible, try to find a candle that complements and connects with the theme of the session. Use music to create an atmosphere of calm and quiet. Include a symbol representing the theme of the session. This will help to make the link between our human experience and our religious experience.

everyone. This helps each person to feel they are part of the group as well as being an equal member of a community in which Jesus is present.

Preparing yourself

The reader should prepare well. For this reason, the scripture reference is included in the notes for the parents, priests and catechists, together with a short commentary. For example, the scripture we have chosen for the session on Belonging (Isaiah 43:1):
"I have called you by your name; you are mine."
We encourage you to read Isaiah 43:1-7 so that you can see this quote in context.

In these verses in Isaiah, God is making it clear that he was claiming Israel and was not going to let her go; God claims us and he is not going to let us go. God is telling us that he knows each of us individually, so much so that he knows our names and claims us as his own. The notes for each session offer suggestions on how the parent, priest or catechist might reflect, by way of preparing themselves for the session. In this first session, for example, you are invited to recall what it means to be precious in someone else's eyes. By reflecting on the scripture passages in this way, you will be better equipped to communicate the message to your participants.

Develop ways of exploring scripture

It is important to develop different mediums through which you can bring the scripture story to life in a way that will engage and sustain attention. Consider the needs, motivations, attention spans and abilities of people with learning disabilities and the challenges presented by them. The following ideas may be helpful:

- Music can communicate and enable learning on a cognitive, emotional and affective level. Many hymns and other religious music can be found on the internet by searching www.youtube.com.
- Drama and role play: masks, finger and hand puppets can provide enjoyable ways of engaging people in scripture.
- Soft cloth toys, fabric wall charts and other representational items and figures, provide sensory stimulation and rewarding and motivating experiences for students with hypo– and/or hypersensitivities and can be used to re-enact scripture stories. (See the EQD website: www.eqd.co.uk. See also sensory toy library websites, such as www.cheapdisabilityaids.co.uk and www.sensorytoywarehouse.com both of which have great inexpensive products.)

- Soft cloth and felt products: materials, toys and novelties can be substantial visual aids through which we can communicate scripture stories, whilst also offering tactile and interactive opportunities to help engage attention.
- PowerPoint presentations: the website sermons4kids (www.sermons4kids.com) has a number of animated PowerPoint presentations which when used for ministry purposes are free.

Draw out the Church's teaching

Each session explores scripture and draws from it the truths of the Catholic faith. This part of the session can be very taxing on those who feel they want to teach rather than to be with, to care rather than to share, to give rather than mutually giving and receiving. There is no place for this in symbolic catechesis. We are companions on a spiritual journey. There is no status, no authority, no instructor. You can be flexible, of course. An activity which suits one person may not engage the attention of another. For example, someone who has a great deal of energy may benefit from a moving activity rather than a sedentary one.

The content of faith must be presented in ways that are age and ability-appropriate, culturally sensitive and varied so as to keep things interesting and fresh. Each session explores the scripture and draws from it the truths of the Catholic faith found in scripture and tradition and in accordance with the teaching authority of the Church. This is done through conversation, by using images and through activities.

Photo: Kim Llewellyn

Reflect:

Where the links are made? In the quiet of our hearts, we hear what God is saying to us. You might use some quiet music (such as Taizé). Remember, what God is saying to each person will differ from person to person. Each session offers ideas for reflection which will help you prepare for the sessions.

When deciding how to draw out the truths of the faith, It is important to remember that the core of our Christian faith is love. Pope Benedict XVI reminds us of this in his first encyclical *Deus Caritas Est* (God is love) by beginning the encyclical with the words: "God is love, and he who abides in love abides in God, and God abides in him" (I John 4:16).

Every session includes references to the *Catechism of the Catholic Church* which invite us to reflect on the Church's teaching. In the first session on Belonging, we refer to the story Jesus told about God as a gatekeeper, and and us as sheep. He said: "The one who enters by the gate is the shepherd of the sheep. The gatekeeper opens the gate for him, and the sheep listen to his voice. He calls his own sheep by name and leads them out."
(John 10:2-3). Jesus was reminding us that God calls each of us by name. The Catechism also tells us that our names are sacred, our names are icons of us which demand respect as a sign of our dignity (CCC 2158, 2159, 2167).

The aim of the activities

Bearing in mind that our main objective is to foster this relationship with a personal loving God, the activities during our sessions aim to:

i. share and build up trust where relationships can form and where a feeling of belonging can develop;
ii. ensure that our activities help to make the transition to the religious dimension. Doing rather than talking here often has a greater impact;
iii. foster an environment which conveys security, love and a lack of criticism; where there is time to share, to look, to enjoy; a feeling of calm, quiet, a time of few words;
iv. People with learning disabilities are often immersed in the present moment, the now. Thus their needs are now, their experiences are now, and whether their communication is verbal or non-verbal, they are always intuitively asking us to go slowly, quieten down, listen and "be with". A person who is agitated and restless desperately needs this quiet, attentive response and acceptance. We must allow time to find that rhythm, to walk at that pace.
Sharing that present moment – being together in the now – we are helped to become aware of each other's gifts and to value them. Gradually, we learn to listen with our spirits as well as our ears. Our companionship and our environment speak to us of God and his presence with us. So the way is paved for our human experience to be linked to the spiritual in the special place.

Step 4: linking God's story with ours; getting the message

We explore the scripture, linking it to our life experience, so that we can see that what God is saying to us is relevant today. God listens to our prayer; God is interested in us and he cares about what is happening in our lives and he cares about us. We use ritual and symbol to make this connection; what we call symbolic catechesis.

Symbolic catechesis

Symbolic catechesis began in the 1950s. A disabled priest, Henri Bissonnier, in Lyons, was teaching in schools of special education and he became obsessed with the education and evangelisation of the weakest. From then on, he taught in the schools of special education at the Catholic University of Paris and at the University of Louvain. He wrote hundreds of articles and a dozen books, which were nourished by his experience, especially in the Bicêtre hospice where he developed a special catechetical training for children and adolescents affected by environmental, psychological and social disabilities. At BICE, he launched the Medico-Social and Psycho-Pedagogic Commission of the International Catholic Child Bureau which propelled him into high international forums travelling to 60 countries.

He had a breakthrough after watching a young dancer perform a religious dance before a Mass for those with special needs. He asked one of the children what the dance meant. She said: "Jesus is with me", and he realised that non-verbal expression is much more open to the understanding of people with learning disabilities. They taught him that the spiritual is not just an abstraction; it allows our total self to be involved.

Bissonier believed that, because they may be unable to use ordinary language, people with learning disabilities find symbols instead, just as we who have language, find symbols when trying to express something abstract; like love, for example. Bissonier distinguised between sign and symbol. "Symbols," he says, conquer reality; they carry the reality in themselves.

Fr Euchariste Paulhus, a French Canadian, was another key figure in the development of symbolic catechesis. He wrote a doctoral thesis on the "Religious Educability" of people with intellectual disabilities. Insights gained from this thesis enabled Fr Jean Mesny of Lyon, France, to develop a symbolic method of catechesis known as *Méthode Vivre* meaning, to live).

His method was based on the concept of the Church as the Body of Christ, with everyone a part of that body. He and Bissonnier had many ideas in common, particularly about the use of symbol and bodily expression. He believed that symbol could touch people very deeply and, he argued that the classical method of teaching people with learning disabilities was nigh impossible because religion is so abstract.

"Jesus is with me" – non-verbal communication through dancing

At that time, Sr Mary Therese Harrington was involved in the same work in Chicago. In 1964, Paulhus and Mesny brought the *Méthode Vivre* to Chicago to work with her.

From 1964 to 1968, the team developed and adopted the *Méthode Vivre*, a catechetical method that used symbols and drew from the individual's experiences. With it, there is a symbolic progression that connects a basic lived experience to a sacred, liturgical experience with the help of gestures and song. The symbolism is not taught but is evoked in phases, movng the individual from one experience to the other.

Symbolic catechesis uses an intuitive approach. Approaches that hint at instruction simply present anyone with a learning disability with yet another obstacle to overcome. Unnecessary or complicated words lose people's attention. With symbolic catechesis, words should be directly related to concrete experience. When questions are asked, for example, they should be simple and only used when a straightforward answer is required. "Do you like these flowers?" calls for a yes or no answer. "Why do you like these flowers?" requires quite a complicated thought process in order to answer.

As this method has developed, we have discovered the importance of symbols and ritual play in helping people with, and without learning disabilities, to get "the message". For instance, you might use newly opened flowers and buds as your symbol in a session on new life. This symbol of how the flower is transformed from the bud into new life is a familiar one and it can be used to provide a link between our human experience of new life, with the mystery of the new life given to us by the Spirit. They see how the bud changes and becomes a beautiful flower and they can be led to see how we change too, when we experience new life in the Spirit. It is a clue to what we do next and prompts anticipation for the next part of the session.

Using our senses

We know how important our five senses are in imparting and receiving information and for drawing out an intuitive response. This is not something new in terms of spirituality. St Augustine fastens upon the five senses to describe his conversion. He heard, saw, smelled, tasted and touched God. Or rather, God took the initiative and spoke to him, shone upon him, shed fragrance about him, touched him and let him taste the divine goodness. This is the way St Augustine expresses his experience of God, that is to say, the saving revelation which broke in and changed Augustine's life (*Confessions* 10. 27).

No other Christian writers have expressed more beautifully the human experience of the divine self-communication than Augustine and John. John opens his first letter by testifying to that revelation which was heard, seen and touched in Jesus Christ. Using the senses is important for all of us; but it is particularly significant to people who do not use cognitive abilities and reasoning to understand the messages directed towards them. It follows then that we must attract those senses and use them to the full. If one of the senses is impaired, it is important to adapt accordingly so as to make up for that loss with increased emphasis on the other four.

When using the senses, do consider the degrees and qualities. A smell may be too intense; a sound can be too piercing or too high-pitched. We are all aware that different types of music may have a very different effect. Martial music is inappropriate when we are in a sacred place but fine on the parade ground. Loud and trendy music with a beat is great at a disco but unhelpful when we are

You might be interested in learning more about the current perspectives on spiritual transformation in theology and Christian spirituality of people with learning disabilities. Check Amazon for books written by and about the work of Jean Vanier.

Photo: Diana Klein

aiming for a quiet, thoughtful environment which will help us to pray. And, sometimes, rather than having to listen to sound at all, we appreciate silence. We've learned how silence allows us to savour, to take in and appreciate what has gone before, the environment we are in, the presence of other people who are sharing the same experience and are united with us. It has an aura of its own. We can focus, allow "the other" to enter so that we may feel the presence of God amongst us and within us.

For people with learning disabilities, the present time is often of more interest and relevance. This involvement in the "now" adds to the intensity of the present experience and draws in all the messages the senses receive. It is really "lived". We should not willingly allow anything to distract from this and take away from the power of the intuitive response. For, it is by intuition we hope that people with learning disabilities will make that leap from the human experience to the mystery of God.

It is also helpful to be aware that participants who have autistic spectrum conditions (ASC) experience particular perceptual processing difficulties which can mean they can be hypo- or maybe hyper-sensitive in relation to input through the different sensory channels. Part of the relationship building and session planning will come from discovering individual preferences and comfort zones. A carefully worded questionnaire to gain information about this prior to programmes beginning can help ensure a positive approach.

Step 5: Responding and celebrating

The group moves again, to a new place where they can relax, celebrate and chat; responding to what they have experienced. To help make the transition, you might incorporate a hymn which you sing or that you listen to; it might be a chant of the sign of peace or quiet music.

We thought about the importance of the transition from the beginning of the session and the activity when we moved into the special place. We are now thinking about the transition from the special place to the place where we will celebrate and reflect with one another on what has happened during the session.

It is important to create a relaxed place where people can share with one another what they have experienced together, and how it will impact, enrich and contribute to their lives. This is a very important part of the session. The celebration might include food, drink, laughter, conversation and, most of all, mutual enjoyment in each other's company. Remember, this may be one of the few opportunities people have of making friends who have similar abilities, similar communication skills and a similar faith. Ensuring the importance of giving people this space where friendships can develop naturally cannot be underestimated. When we talk about celebrating, ideas of joy, fun, rejoicing, music and dance come to mind. They may say the session was good, how they enjoyed the activity, how it felt to pray, to hear Jesus speaking to them, or you may see a degree of their engagement in their facial expressions.

At the end of the session

The goodbyes should be made as personal as the rest of the session with a looking-forward to the next meeting. At the end of a session, you might think about giving everyone a memento, a "God be with you" which echoes the theme of the day. It helps people recall the session and acts as a concrete symbol, a reminder of what they've experienced during their time together, which they can savour for many days to come and it keeps the session alive. A "goodbye song" provides another opportunity to acknowledge and celebrate the presence and contribution of each person as their name is sung.

Using the materials

These materials attempt to provide for a range of needs and abilities, from those with profound and multiple learning disabilities to those who may be able to use symbol supported texts, to those who may have only some level of verbal communication. We have attempted to provide materials that will empower parents, priests and catechists with ideas they can use and personalise in the faith formation of people with learning disabilities.

Each session begins by telling you the aim of the session. Make sure you understand this and that you keep it in mind as you go through the session. It is the point you are trying to make. The aim will be repeated in a simplified way at the beginning of the session. The oldest chestnut in public speaking advice is to "tell people what you're going to say, say it, and then tell them what you said". By doing this, you will communicate what the session aims to communicate.

Parents, priests and catechists who are inexperienced can sometimes be tempted to become distracted by the activity or the music or whatever, especially if the candidate

A Resource Pack to enable participation of people with learning disabilities is available on the St Joseph's Pastoral Centre website (www.stjoseph.org.uk/) free of charge. It contains templates for Widgit cards to help engage people in responding and sharing with one another. The cards have been used throughout the materials as part of the sessions; but for a full explanation of the resource, see the Appendix.

is enjoying that; they then miss making the point of the session. Remember that the purpose of the activity is to make a link with the religious dimension (the scripture) and to help the candidate get the message of the session. Where possible, we have tried to include more than one activity to meet the needs for a range of abilities. These materials are not intended to be prescriptive. They do not propose to tell you what to do step-by-step. Rather, they are intended to make you think about how to communicate with your candidate. They are meant to empower you to get ideas that will work with your candidate. For example:

- In one session, we suggest that you use finger puppets to tell the scripture story. If you find that this works well with your candidate, consider making them a frequent part of mediating scripture.
- You might use the book to lead you through the faith formation process; or you may use it to inform yourself on one way of doing it and adapt it as needed.
- You might give your candidate an activity book photocopied from the additional resources CD; you may adapt it and personalise it; or you might make up your own activities. Activities are suggested for each session, together with ideas you might like to use to make up a book.

Icon of Christ, the Teacher of Enlightenment

A word of warning when it comes to personalising these materials. You can only do what you can do. Do your best and trust the Holy Spirit to do the rest. Remember the aim of catechesis is to come to know the person of Christ and desire to be his followers. Ask yourself two most important questions:
(1) when you are planning the session: "Will this session help people to know Jesus a little better?"
(2) When you finish it: "Do the people who have been in this session know Jesus a little better?"

Allow the words of Pope John Paul II to echo in your heart:

"The definitive aim of catechesis is to put people not only in touch but in communion, in intimacy, with Jesus Christ. Only he can lead us to the love of the Father in the Spirit and make us share in the life of the Holy Trinity."

Catechesi Tradendae
(on Catechesis in our time), 5

Symbols
of faith

— Section 1 —

Baptised in the name of the Father, Son and Holy Spirit

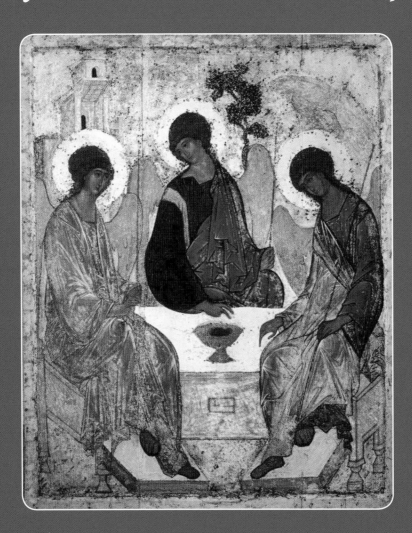

1. Belonging to God

 Session aim
To discover that, just as we belong to our families or our communities and they call us by name, we belong to God's family and God calls each of us by name.

Preparing for the session

In this session, the essential message we want to communicate is that God calls each of us by name; we belong to him. Belonging is one of the needs common to us all. We experience belonging in our families, with our friends and in our communities. In the places where we belong, we are called by our names. Only the people who know us can call us by our name; others do not know our name. Read this passage from Isaiah as you prepare for the session.

Isaiah 43:1-7

1 *"But now thus says the LORD, He who created you,*
   O Jacob, He who formed you, O Israel:
   Do not fear, for I have redeemed you;
   I have called you by your name, you are mine.
2 *When you pass through the waters,*
   I will be with you; and through the rivers,
   they shall not overwhelm you;
   when you walk through fire, you shall not be burned
   and the flame shall not consume you.
3 *For I am the LORD your God, the Holy One of Israel,*
   your Saviour. I give Egypt as your ransom,
   Ethiopia and Seba in exchange for you.
4 *Because you are precious in my sight,*
   and honoured, and I love you.
   I give people in return for you,
   nations in exchange for your life.
5 *Do not fear, for I am with you;*
   I will bring your offspring from the east,
   and from the west I will gather you;

Reminder:

There is a CD of additional resources in the back cover of this book, which provides you with ready-made pages to complement the sessions in this book.

Facing page:
Icon by Andrei Rublev depicting the Holy Trinity

⁶ *I will say to the north, 'Give them up.'*
and to the south, 'Do not withhold;
bring my sons from far away and my daughters from the end of the earth
⁷ *everyone who is called by my name, whom I created*
for my glory, whom I formed and made.'"

In these verses, God is making it pretty clear that he was claiming Israel and was not going to let her go. Notice the ascending descriptions of ownership from creation (matter made from nothing), to forming Israel out of this matter, then rescuing Israel from captivity (the redeeming), and finally calling her by her name. God is speaking to us not like a king on a throne pronouncing an edict, but like someone who loves us so much, his heart is bursting.

Just as parents long for the day their child is born, when they can call their child by name, so God, who seems to have waited an eternity to call Israel by her name and, in this act of speaking her name, claims Israel as his own: "You are mine." God goes on to tell Israel: "You are precious in my eyes and I love you." In this reading, God is telling us that he knows each of us individually, so much so that he knows our names and claims us as his own.

By way of preparing yourself for this session, you might reflect on what it means to be really precious in someone's eyes. The sense of being precious in God's eyes is something you are trying to communicate to the participants.

The Catechism

Our names are sacred, our names are icons of us which demand respect as a sign of our dignity. The Catechism supports the theological input of this session. The Catechism reminds us that God calls us by name and says it is the icon of the person. It demands respect as a sign of the dignity of the one who bears it (CCC 2158, 2167).

Leading the session

When you introduce people to this session, you might say something like: "Today's session is all about belonging." You might begin by exploring with the participants what they belong to and what belongs to them. You can prompt them by showing them a picture of a parent and child. Point out that the parent belongs to the child and the child belongs to the parent. Some people might find it easier to symbolise what they belong to or what belongs to them by using mime or dancing, or acting out how they belong to their families with images or with dolls. Make sure you find ways to communicate in the way your participant can. This part of the session begins to open up the content of the session.

Welcome

Every session begins with the welcome of each person by name, but in this session this is especially important: (1) because it is the first time you are gathering and (2) because we are reflecting on how God calls each of us by name.

The human dimension
(the activity drawing on our life experience)

The activity we suggest in this session is to make name tags. Encourage people to think about how their names belong to them as they make the name tags by explaining how our name tags will tell others what to call us. These tags can be reused in the following sessions. Ask the participants if they like being called by their names. When everyone has finished, you are ready to move to the special place. Invite people to bring their name tag as the symbol for this session, the symbol of belonging, and put it on the focal point.

The religious dimension
(in the special place where Jesus speaks to us)

Don't rush when you move from your meeting place to your special place. Take your time and consider using music to create an atmosphere for the next part of the session. Invite people to carry their name tags from one place to the other and to place them on the focal point. You might use quiet music to help people shift their mood from being active to being reflective. For example, David Evans' "Be still for the presence of the Lord, the holy one is here", or something relating to the theme of the session like David Haas', "You are mine" based on Isaiah 49:15-16.

Lighting the candle

We light the candle to remind us that Jesus is the light in our lives and he is here with us. This time will become the signal that a new phase of the session is beginning. This helps to calm and refocus people and

You might think about asking the participants' (or their carers) to bring photos of parents' and children to make this sense of belonging more personal.

It is helpful when engaging people with severe or profound disabilities in making name tags to offer a variety of brightly coloured or different textured cards so that participation in the activity begins with the invitation to choose colours and materials; then provide a variety of stickers and decorating materials for those who cannot colour in or write their names. If writing or reading names is not something people can do, consider using a photo instead of writing a name.

it is another way to help promote a reflective atmosphere; it will shift the mood and help people enter into the religious experience.

Greeting the scripture

Remember the suggestion in the introduction which works for both the Old Testament and New Testament readings for children using the tune of "London Bridge": We have come to hear God's word, hear God's word, hear God's word. We have come to hear God's word, let us listen! You may want to use something different for adults depending on their abilities. For example, you might sing Linda Stassen's "Sing Alleluia to the Lord". It is easy to learn and most people can sing it. Alternatively, use an acclamation used in your parish that people know. Emphasise that we are greeting the Gospel, the Good News, and we sing out of joy.

Sign our heads, our mouths and our hearts

A boy, fascinated by the candle, is led into deep prayer

Introduce the practice of signing our heads, mouths and hearts because we hear God's Word in our heads, proclaim it with our mouths and feel it in our hearts.

Children's Liturgy Mill Hill Dec 2004, photographer Diana Klein

Listening to Jesus in the scripture

Holding the book, read the scripture clearly and reverently to the whole group using this (or another) adapted version of Isaiah 43:1-7.

But now the LORD says, I created you, I formed you,
do not fear, for I've saved you;
I have called you by your name, you are mine.
When you pass through rivers,
I will be with you and I will keep you safe.
When you walk through fire, I will not let you be burned
For I am your God, the Holy One.
You are precious in my sight and I love you.
Do not be afraid, I am always with you.

Giving the scripture message to each person

Now approach each member of the group individually, holding their hands and looking into their eyes, saying: "[Name] Jesus tells us today that God, his Father, has called you by your name; you are his."

Reading the scripture again to the whole group

After each person has heard Jesus speaking to them, the message is then given to the whole group again. This is done with a wide gesture, which includes everyone and helps each person to feel they are part of the group and community in which God is present.

Breaking the scripture open

Take the name tags from the focal point and present them to the participants. Use music to help create an atmosphere where they can hear God calling them by name. For example, you might play Bernadette Farrell's "You have called us by our name, we belong to you" while you give each person their name tag. If any of your participants are deaf, you might sign the words to the music. If you have facilities to watch a DVD, the Farrell CD shows this song in sign language. You are trying to help people hear God calling them by name. You might pause the music, or the signing from time to time to call each person forward to present them with their name tag.

Getting the message

The idea that God calls each and every one of us by name is an awesome thought for all of us, so give people time to hear God saying that to them. Bring this part of the session to a close by thanking God for this time together and invite them to move to your celebration place.

Sharing the message/celebrating

It is time to have refreshments, where people can share with one another what they have experienced in the session as they reflected on how God calls them each by name, how we belong to him. What do they have to say about this? Give them time to respond to this question. If people can read, you might have a set of cards with everyone's names. You might ask them to find their name and put it into a basket. Or, you might ask them to pick someone else's name (or, if they don't read, their photo), and place it in the basket as they thank God for the gift of that person. Alternatively, people might go around the group calling each person by name and shaking their hand.

Causeway Prospects produce music especially for worship with people with disabilities. The song "The Father himself loves you" is a good example.

Note:
For people who have difficulty in listening to a long Gospel, you might cut it down, for example: "The LORD says, I created you, I formed you. I have called you by your name, you are mine. You are precious in my sight and I love you." Use your judgement—as long as you are true to the message of the scripture.

✓ **Remember, for this session, you will need:**

✓ **To introduce the session:**
Pictures of the families to invite discussion about belonging.

✓ **Activity and symbolism:**
• A name label made of card with each person's name (or photo);
• Crayons, coloured pens, ribbon and/or clips or holders with a variety of brightly coloured or different textured cards;
• A variety of stickers and decorative materials for those who cannot colour in or write their names.

✓ **For the special place:**
• The holy book with the simplified reading placed inside it, an icon of Christ, the name tags you have made and/or the photographs of their families that they have brought, draped cloth and a candle.

✓ **Music:**
• All but one of which can be heard on YouTube. In addition, most of them have videos you can show if you have a projector and laptop:
• David Evans' "Be still for the presence of the Lord. The holy one is here";
• David Haas' "You are mine" based on Isaiah 49:15-16;
• Bernadette Farrell's "You Have Called Us by our name, we belong to you". The CD includes a signed version of this song;
• Linda Stassen's "Sing Alleluia to the Lord";
• Gerald Markland's "Do not be afraid, for I have called you by your name; you are mine";
• Causeway Prospect, "The Father himself loves you" (not available on YouTube), see www.prospects.org.uk/

2. Belonging to Jesus

We are marked with the cross at our baptism to show that we belong to Jesus.

Preparing for the session

In this session, we will continue to explore the concept of belonging, first by looking at the things that belong to us (our books, our rooms, our houses, our clothing) and how we mark them to show that they are ours. We will then have a simplified rite of baptism and we will see how we are marked with the sign of the cross and claimed by Christ to show we belong to him.

You might have a selection of signs and tags to show how we label the things that belong to us. Draw on people's personal experience of marking their belongings. For example, you might ask what chaos there would be at the end of the day at school if none of the coats were labelled and nobody knew whose coat was whose.

There are many examples you can draw upon to explore people's life experiences. In preparation for this session, you might ask the participants or their carers to bring an item of clothing or a book which has been marked with their name.

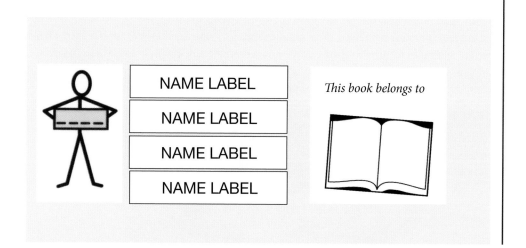

John 15:5. 10-14

[5] *"I am the vine, you are the branches.*
Those who abide in me and I in them bear much fruit,
because apart from me you can do nothing.
[10] *If you keep my commandments,*
you will abide in my love, just as I have kept my Father's
commandments and abide in his love.
[11] *I have said these things to you so that my joy*
may be in you and that your joy may be complete.
[12] *"This is my commandment, that you*
love one another as I have loved you.
[13] *No one has greater love than this,*
to lay down one's life for one's friends.
[14] *You are my friends if you do what I command you."*

In these verses, Jesus explains to his disciples that, apart from him, they can do nothing; but if they live in him and he lives in them they will bear much fruit. The fruit of the vine is love for one another. Love for one another prolongs the love that Jesus has for his disciples, and this continues the Father's love for him. This love is the life the Father shares with Jesus, and he with his disciples and with us. It is not a passing emotion; it is a way of living and being connected to Christ, just as the branches are connected to the vine and they draw their goodness from the vine.

Once again, we reflect on the way God (in Jesus) speaks to us not like the Messiah that he is; but like someone who loves us as good friends love one another. We are like him when we are willing to do anything for our friends, to sacrifice for them, to love them "warts and all". This is the kind of love Jesus is calling us to because, in our baptism, Jesus has claimed us for his own; we were anointed so that we can become more like him.

By way of preparing yourself for this session, you might reflect on what it means to be that kind of friend. Thank God for the times when you have experienced that selfless love for someone or from someone.

The Catechism

The baptised have "put on Christ". Through the Holy Spirit, baptism is a bath that purifies, justifies, and sanctifies (Gal. 3:27; 1 Cor 6:11) (CCC1227). This concept of "putting on Christ" is something you might reflect on by asking yourself what happens when we put on a uniform or a football kit. We are marked with the identity of the school, a company or a team. You might consider exploring that concept with your participants if you have time.

Leading the session

Welcome

As always, each person should be welcomed by name. If possible, let them wear the name tags they made in the first session. Talk about how we continue to talk about belonging today. This session is all about belonging to Jesus. We were marked (or we will be marked) by the cross at our baptism to show that we belong to him.

The human dimension
(the activity drawing on our life experience)

Our activity in this session is to explore what happens at a baptism. You might do this by acting out a simplified baptism or, depending on the ability of your candidates, you might get them to colour in a picture of a baptism. Tell them it will help them to better understand why we make the sign of the cross on ourselves. If you are colouring in a picture of baptism, you can use the one in the activity book from the CD. If you are acting out a baptism, you will need:

- Someone to play the role of the priest. He has the biggest speaking part so choose someone who will be able to cope;
- Parents, godparents and guests. The parents should decide whether the baby is a girl or boy and should think of a name;
- A bowl of water, a small bowl of oil, a white blanket, a candle and a baby doll.

Note:

If you are working with people who are on the autistic spectrum, be aware that you may have to explain this in a different way. They will find it difficult to conceive of the idea of "putting on Christ" because of the literal way they see things.

You might want or need to simplify this baptism for some candidates, who may find this exercise too long and too complicated. Always keep in mind that people process information in different ways and at different levels. So, you may want to keep your sentences much shorter and simpler. For example:
Priest: Welcome! What is the baby's name? I am going to make a cross on his/her head to say he/she belongs to Jesus. Then, I am going to pour water on the baby's head.
I am going to tell the baby that Jesus wants to be his/her friend. Now I will give the baby a candle. It is like giving Jesus to him/her because we believe that Jesus is our light [replace the word 'baby' with 'person' if appropriate].

You can act out the baptism using this text or you can improvise:

Priest:	"Welcome, everyone, to the baptism of this child." To the parents, he says: "What name have you chosen for your child?"
Parents:	(Say the name)
Priest:	"What do you ask for your child?"
Parents:	"Baptism."
Priest:	"[Name of the baby], the Christian community welcomes you with great joy. I am now going to mark you with a cross on your forehead as a sign that you belong to Jesus."
Priest:	"Do you want your child to become a member of the Christian family, to belong to Jesus?"
Parents:	"Yes."
Priest:	(To the parents:) "It will be your job to teach your child to know Jesus and bring him or her to church. Will you do that?"
Parents:	"Yes."
Priest:	(To the godparents:) "Are you willing to help these parents in this important job?"
Godparents:	"Yes."
Priest:	(Putting a touch of oil on the child's breast,) "May Jesus give you strength." Then, blessing the water by making a sign of the cross over it, says: "Bless this water. It will be used for this child's baptism." (The priest then turns to all present.) He says: "Do you believe in God the Creator?"
All:	"Yes, we do."
Priest:	"Do you believe in Jesus, his son, who claims us as his own?"
All:	"Yes, we do."
Priest:	(To the parents:) "Do you want your child to believe these things?"
Parents:	"Yes, we do."
Priest:	(To the godparents:) "Do you promise to help take care of this child, and to help teach him/her about Jesus?"
Godparents:	"Yes, we do."
Priest:	(Pouring water over the child's head,) "I baptise you in the name of the Father, and of the Son and of the Holy Spirit."
All:	"Amen."
Priest:	(Uses the oil to make the sign of the cross on the child's head and says:) "May you live like Jesus." He then places the white blanket on the child (With the parents' and godparents' help) and says: "Receive this white

	garment. It Is sign that you will live forever."
Parents:	(Light the candle and hand it to the child or hold it for them.)
Priest:	"Receive the light of Christ. Parents, God has given you the job of keeping this light alive. May the child walk in the light always."

An alternative activity

Acting out this baptism may just be too difficult for some people. If this is the case or if your candidate has a preference for making things, you might copy this line drawing (which you will find in the activity materials) or find a clip-art version and ask them to colour it in. They can paste it into their acvitity book alongside a photo of their baptism if they have one.

We are now ready to go to our special place.

drawing by Kim Blundeel © 2014

Some of these concepts are likely to be difficult to share with people with learning disabilities; but, I'd like to offer a little further explanation on two points:

1. When we are anointed with the oil of chrism, we are made Christ-like, we are given a share in the priestly, prophetic and royal ministry of Jesus. (That carries the expectation that we will proclaim God's word, we will tell people what God is like and we will care for one another.)

2. The white garment is a sign of being a new Christian; but it is more than that. It is the uniform of heaven. We share in eternal life now through our baptism.

The religious dimension
(in the special place where Jesus speaks to us)

As people move to the special place, make a ritual of carrying the lighted candle and placing it carefully on the focal point. You might consider playing the chorus of "Water of Life" by Stephen Dean: "Water of Life, cleanse and refresh us, raise us to life in Christ Jesus!" is very easy to learn and it can be sung over and over again until everyone has settled in the special place.

If you choose to use this music, it can replace the Gospel acclamation. On this occasion, too, the candle is already lit, but tell people that it reminds us that Jesus is the light in our lives and he is here with us as we shift our mood and enter into the religious experience.

Sign our heads, mouths and hearts

We sign our heads, mouths and hearts to show we hear God's word in our heads, proclaim it with our mouths and feel it in our hearts.

Listening to Jesus in the scripture

Holding the book, read the scripture clearly and reverently to the whole group using this (or another) adapted version of John 15:5. 10-14.

> Jesus said to his disciples: "I love you just as God loves me.
> Live in my love. If you do as I say,
> you are living in my love. This is what I say:
> that you love one another as I have loved you.
> There is no greater love than to give your life for your friends.
> And you are my friends if you do what I tell you.
> I am telling you to do this: love one another."

Giving the scripture message to each person

Now approach each member of the group individually, holding their hands and looking into their eyes, saying:

> "[Name] Jesus tells you today: I love you. You belong to me."

Reading the scripture again to the whole group.

After each person has heard Jesus speaking to them, the message is then given to the whole group again. This is done with a wide gesture, which includes everyone and helps each person to feel they are part of the group and community in which God is present.

Breaking the scripture open

Invite people to come forward to dip their fingers into the bowl of water and to make the sign of the cross on themselves, perhaps one at a time. You might play the chorus of "Water of Life" again as they do so.

Depending on the ability of your participants, you might then ask each participant to finish this sentence: "Jesus is my friend and I want to do as he says and love everyone by being…" Jesus asks each and every one of us to be like him, to be loving, sharing, caring.

There are symbol supported text lotto games on the Widgit website called 'Being more like Jesus'. Google 'symbol supported text cards', or download some images of people engaged in loving, sharing and caring activities. These can be used for cutting and sticking or for choosing as part of a song activity. Something that might work with children would be: "Kerry says we can help our friends × 3 as we grow more like Jesus (to the tune of "Skip to my Lou").

We use our hands to mark ourselves with the cross to remind us that we belong to Jesus. He wants us to use our hands to be like him by helping one another, looking after one another and comforting one another.

Getting the message

Give people time to hear what Jesus is saying to them today. Watch carefully if they share their message with you. Value what they have to say, and don't be surprised by it. Bring this part of the session to a close with a prayer. Children (and some adults) may like to sing this part of the well-known song "Jesus loves me" repeating it two or three times:

"Jesus loves me, this I know 'cause the bible tells me so."

Depending on your participants, you might like to listen to the hymn, "I come to the garden". I think the refrain would work very well by changing a few words, as follows: "Jesus walks with me, and he talks with me, and he tells me I am His own; and the joy we share as we tarry here, none other has ever known."

You are now ready to move to the place where you will celebrate.

Sharing the message/celebrating

It's time to celebrate, to share the Good News with one another. It is time to have refreshments, where people can share with one another what this time together has been like for them. In baptism, we come to belong to Jesus. He likes to celebrate so don't leave him out! Invite him to be with you; talk to him, share with him, celebrate with him, and ask the others to help him feel welcome too. You might make some cards describing what Jesus is like: loving, caring, sharing, good friend, good listener. You might have matching cards with similar words describing how we can be like Jesus. You might ask people to match the cards to show everyone how they can be like him.

✔ **Remember, for this session, you will need:**

✔ **To introduce the session:**
Name tags from the first session, signs to show house numbers, labels to identify their belongings, their houses, etc.

✔ **Activity and special place:**
• A bowl of water, a small bowl of oil, a white blanket, a baptism candle, a baby doll, and, as always, the holy book with the simplified reading placed inside, an icon of Christ and a draped cloth. For the sharing: the card game.

✔ **Music which can all be heard on YouTube.**
• Stephen Dean: "Water of Life" Sheet music can be ordered on line: www.printandpraise. com/songpr...971/107255.img
• Sr Virginia Vissing, SSMN singing "Abba Father" (especially the verse "You will give me living water").
• "Jesus loves me": sheet music for this is available free on the Making Music Fun website, http://www.makingmusicfun.net/htm/f_printit_free_printable_sheet_music/jesus-loves-me-sheet-music.htm.
• Simon Leyton, C. Austin Miles, "I come to the garden".

3. Living in the Holy Spirit

Session aim To get a sense of God living in us through the Holy Spirit — who helps us bring Jesus' love to everyone.

Preparing for the session

In the first session, we said that God, our Father in heaven, calls each of us by name, he tells us that we are his. We referred to God, as Jesus' Father and our Father in heaven. The Holy Spirit unites the three persons of the Trinity in a community of love.

In the last session, we talked about how we were marked with the cross to show that we belong to Jesus, and we invited people to make the sign of the cross on themselves. We focused on Jesus and said that he asks each and every one of us to be like him: to be loving, sharing, caring. We said that he wants us to help one another, to look after one another, to comfort one another.

In this session, we hear about how the Holy Spirit helps us to be like Jesus, to do the things he wants us to do as his followers. It is not easy to express something abstract like love. Wind, fire or a dove are some of the symbols we use to describe the Holy Spirit. The picture to the right is the earliest known depiction of the Trinity. I'm not sure which of these figures is the Father, the Son or the Spirit, but it tells us that people have been trying to express the Trinity for a long time. You might ask people to show you what they think love looks like. Some will draw a heart or give you a hug or a kiss. IKEA sells a "hug pillow". It's a heart shaped pillow with arms outstretched that can give a hug. Remember, it is important to listen to what people have to say verbally or non-verbally; it helps them open up to the content of the session.

The earliest known depiction of the Trinity. This is the far end of the work with Trinity resurrecting Lazarus. *Dogmatic Sarcophagus*, 350 AD Vatican Museums.

Paul's letter to the Romans 8:14-17

[14] *For all who are led by the Spirit of God*
are children of God.
[15] *For you did not receive a spirit of slavery*
to fall back into fear, but you have received
a spirit of adoption.
When we cry, "Abba! Father!"
[16] *It is that very Spirit bearing witness*
with our spirit that we are children of God.
[17] *And if children, then heirs,*
heirs of God and joint heirs with Christ—
if, in fact, we suffer with him
so that we may also be glorified with him.

The name "Abba" is more like our word "Daddy". It is a word in Hebrew that shows a close, intimate relationship. You might sign "Abba, Father" (even if you don't have any deaf people in the group). Signing can be a very powerful way to communicate.

In this reading, we focus on how God acts in our lives, as our Father and, like parents in human families, God teaches his children to be like him. We do not have adequate language for God because God is beyond any image we may have; but Jesus told the disciples, if they could see him, they could see the Father (John 14:8-11). We can only know and experience God by coming to know Jesus Christ. Jesus shares with us his experience of God, as creator, as redeemer, and as a person of intimate relationship.

Our experience of this relationship is the Spirit of God living in us. St Paul is telling us that because we are led by the Holy Spirit, and because we are brothers and sisters of Christ, we are children of God. Like Jesus, we too can enjoy the intimate relationship with God, and like Jesus, we can call God "Abba, Father".

By way of preparing yourself for this session, take some time to reflect on what it means to be led by someone. Think about the times when your parent (or a parent-figure), a teacher, a priest or friend has led you to an insight or has guided you in the right direction. Perhaps you are aware of times when the Holy Spirit guided you; those times when the Spirit has put words in your mouth when you didn't know what to say, times when you found courage you didn't think you had in the face of a moral dilemma. Spend some time praying to the Holy Spirit.

The Catechism

The Catechism reminds us of the prayer the bishop says when he invokes the Holy Spirit to be our helper and guide at confirmation:

> "Send your Holy Spirit upon them and give them
> the spirit of wisdom and understanding,
> the spirit of right judgment and courage,
> the spirit of knowledge and reverence.
> Fill them with the spirit of wonder and awe
> in your presence."
>
> (CCC 1299/Rite of Confirmation)

A few paragraphs later in the Catechism, we are reminded that Jesus has marked Christians with the seal of his Spirit by clothing us with power from on high so that we may be his witness (CCC 1303; cf. Lk 24:48-49).

Leading the session

Welcome

Every session begins with the welcome of each person by name. Once again, in this session, we focus on names as we make the sign of the cross "in the name of the Father and of the Son and of the Holy Spirit". Welcome people with an enthusiastic: "Welcome [name]. It is good to see you today!" Say that in this session, we will be learning about another name we use in the sign of the cross, the Holy Spirit. You might ask if anyone knows what the Holy Spirit looks like. Ask too, if anyone knows what love looks like. Show people a drawing of a heart or, perhaps the photograph of a heart sold in Ikea with arms that can reach out to hug you.

The human dimension
(the activity drawing on our life experience)

In this session, we suggest you depict the Trinity in some way. You might print out images of the cross and the Holy Spirit (from the internet) and put them in your activity book or you might draw images using paints or crayons. One group made a Holy Spirit out of

When asking what love looks like, what the Holy Spirit looks like, you might find it helpful to provide some multi-sensory, interactive heart symbols to provide interest and pleasure for those who can participate at an experiential level. (Such items can often be found in charity shops and discount stores in the lead up to Valentine's Day.)

paper maché (but you could equally use clay or plasticine). They then made a cross out of two pieces of wood and used colourful fabric as a background. The idea was that the fabric was like the sky reminding them of God the Father in heaven. During the activity, remind people that when they make the sign of the cross on themselves, they use three names: Father, Son and Holy Spirit.

As people move to the special place, make a ritual of carrying the images of the cross and the Holy Spirit and placing them carefully on the focal point (which should already be set up with the background fabric you choose to use). You might consider singing Sr. Virginia Vissing's first verse of "Abba, Father". It includes Father, Son and Spirit and it's easy to learn:

The photos on these two pages are from the inclusion project at Oakwood with St Joseph's

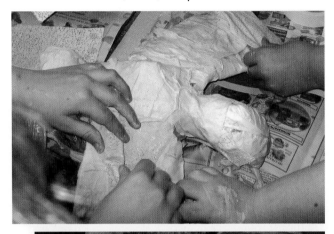

"Abba, Father, send your Spirit,
Glory, Jesus Christ.
Abba, Father, send your Spirit,
Glory, Jesus Christ.
Glory hallelujah, glory, Jesus Christ
Glory hallelujah, glory, Jesus Christ"

Keep in mind that you are trying to help the participants make a link between the special place and the Trinity:

- God, our Father, up in heaven
- the cross as the symbol of Jesus and
- the dove as a symbol of the Holy Spirit

The religious dimension
(in the special place where Jesus speaks to us)

Lighting the candle

We light the candle to remind us that Jesus is the light in our lives and he is here with us. Remember, this is the signal that a new phase of the session is beginning and it helps to shift the mood and help people enter into the religious experience.

Photo: Tunnell

60

Greeting the scripture

You might repeat "Abba, Father" to greet the scripture.

Signing heads, mouths and hearts

Remind people why we do this.

Listening to Jesus in the scripture

Holding the book, read the scripture clearly and reverently to the whole group using this (or another) adapted version of St Paul's letter to the Romans 8:14-17:

> Brothers and sisters, all of us who are led
> by the Holy Spirit are children of God.
> We have been adopted by God
> and when we pray, "Abba, Father",
> the Holy Spirit is in our own spirit
> telling us that we are truly God's children,
> and, if we really believe that,
> we know we are Jesus' brothers and sisters
> and we can call God, "Abba, Father".

Giving the message to each person

Now approach each member of the group individually, holding their hands and looking into their eyes, saying,

> "[Name] Jesus says:
> 'The Holy Spirit is in us and helps us
> to bring God's love to everyone.'"

Now, read the scripture again to the whole group

As always, after each person has heard Jesus speaking to them, the message is then given to the whole group again.

Breaking the scripture open

I suggest that you invite people together as a group to make the sign of the cross on themselves. Remind them how God the Father, Jesus and the Holy Spirit love one another, like a family or a community of love. The Holy Spirit can help us to love one another if we ask. Ask people where they experience love. Is it in their families? Is it in their parishes? Is it in this faith sharing group? Ask them if they will now ask Holy Spirit to help them be more loving.

Getting the message

Give people time to hear what Jesus is saying to them today. Bring this part of the session to a close with some quiet music to help them reflect on how and where they experience love. Daniel Iverson's "Spirit of the living God" might work well.

> "Spirit of the living God, fall afresh on me (×2),
> Break me, melt me, mould me, fill me. Spirit of the living God, fall afresh on me."

Sharing the message/celebrating

Celebrate how special it is to belong to this community of love. Ask if they see this as a place where they experience love; where they are hopefully making new friends. Ask if it is a good place to come; encourage people to thank God for the gift of these friendships and what that is like for them. Carey Landry's "Thank you God" might incorporate what you are trying to do here. "Thank you Lord for giving us life (×3) right where we are. Alleluia, Praise the Lord ×3 right where we are." The next verses replace the word "life" with "love, joy, us". Invite people to add verses thanking God for whatever or whoever they want to.

 Remember, for this session, you will need:

 To introduce the session:
Drawings of hearts, images of doves.

 For the activity and special place:
- Crayons, paints or plasticine, scissors.
- If you choose to use paper maché, you will need flour, water and paper. One method for making it which is cheap and produces a nice and smooth result: one part flour to five parts water; boil about three minutes and let cool. Make the shape (skeleton) of a dove (body, head, wings and tail) using bendable wire or sticks and glue or tape it together. Cover your dove with no more than four layers of paper maché. You might tell the group just to use two layers as they usually overlap more than they should. Let dry *completely*. Then, once again cover with no more than four layers and continue this process until it's as solid as you want it.
- You will also need the holy book with the simplified reading placed inside, draped cloth, a candle.

✓ **Music which is on YouTube:**
- "Spirit of the living God" by Daniel Iverson.
- "Abba Father" by Sr Virginia Vissing SSMN, first verse, "Abba, Father, send your Spirit".
- "Thank you God" by Carey Landry.

The church is a building;
the Church is the people of God

South facade of the Church of St Simeon Stylites, Syria
It is one of the oldest surviving church buildings in the world, dating back to the fifth century

4. The church is a holy place

 Session aim — To help people become aware of the special (sacred) things in the church (God's house) making it a place of prayer.

Preparing for the session

In this session, we will be exploring the church building. The focus of the session is to understand that the church is God's house; it is a holy place, a place where we come to pray, a place where we thank God for all we have and all we are. Our image below is a very modern church, but you might have pictures from older churches and cathedrals, and, if possible, from the participants' own parishes.

Think about how you prepare when a visitor is coming to your house. You probably tidy up before they come; you want the house to look its best for when you welcome them, and you want there to be a good atmosphere when they come. You might have some cakes or biscuits to share with your visitor.

Our Lady and St Vincent Parish, Potters Bar. This church was chosen specially for its clean lines: something much appreciated by people on the autistic spectrum

John 2:14-16

The scripture we have chosen for this session is the story of Jesus finding people in the temple, the money changers and the people who were buying and selling cattle, sheep and pigeons.

¹⁴ *Then he went up to Jerusalem. In the temple,*
   he found people selling cattle, sheep and doves
   and the money changers seated at their tables .
¹⁵ *Making a whip of cords,*
   He drove all of them out of the temple,
   both the sheep and the cattle.
   He also poured out the coins of the money changers
   and overturned their tables.
¹⁶ *He told those who were selling the doves:*
   "Take these things out of here!
   Stop making my Father's house a market place".

Jesus was angry that people were desecrating the holy place. He made a whip and ran about, knocking over the tables of the money changers, spilling coins on the ground. He drove the exchangers out of the area, along with the men selling pigeons and cattle. He also prevented people from using the court as a shortcut. As he cleansed the temple of greed and profit, Jesus quoted from Isaiah 56:7: "My house shall be called a house of prayer." The disciples and others present were in awe of Jesus' authority in God's sacred place.

I chose this reading because of the emphasis on respecting the temple or the church as a holy place, a place of prayer, the aim of this session.

The Catechism

The Catechism tells us that all the signs in the liturgical celebrations are related to Christ, who is glorified in them. Following the tradition of the Catholic Church, we believe that, like the figure of the precious and life-giving cross, holy images of Christ are to be exhibited in churches and on sacred vessels. (CCC 1161).

By way of preparing yourself for this session, take some time to reflect on what the church building means to you. In the early twentieth century, Catholic immigrants to England made enormous financial sacrifices to build the best churches they could. It was important for them to have somewhere beautiful to worship to make somewhere worthy to be called God's house. What are your feelings when you come into a church? Do you sense the divine presence in the church?

Leading the session

Welcome

Every session begins with the welcome of each person by name. In this session, we will be exploring how the church is a holy place. Use the pictures of churches you've brought and tell people the names of the churches. Ask if they know the name of their parish. Ask them how they prepare for visitors, what special things they need.

The human dimension
(the activity drawing on our life experience)

In this session, we are going to explore our experience of being in church. How you do this will depend on the abilities of the people involved, including your own abilities and budget to create images, and so on. Begin by asking what people can tell you about the different things they find in a church. To engage them, here are some ideas:

1. See the pictures on the next page of a church showing some of the things they can find in it. Using the template in the additional resources CD, get them to cut out the items such as the altar, the tabernacle, the lectern, and place them on the sanctuary where they belong. You might like to talk them through the exercise explaining what each of the items is and why it helps to make the church a sacred place.
2. Better still, use this idea and personalise it by taking pictures of the participants' parishes. This option could then be used for other exercises during this programme and in the future.
3. If you and your participants are computer literate, you can create a church with individual items that they can lift and place into the church.
4. See also www.booksatpress.co.uk to access free videos of Puddles the cat visiting a church in Wales and Carlisle Cathedral. Both of these ideas are helpful and fun. It is up to you to find the right idea.

© John Green

Sacred Heart and Mary Immaculate Church, Mill Hill

© Diana Klein

Our Lady and St Vincent, Potters Bar

Moving to the special place

The church can be the special place in this session. You may already be in the church for the activity. If so, move to your focal point by processing with the pictures they have made of the church and place them carefully on it. I suggest using Terry Coelho's "Father we adore you" to create the mood:

> "Father we adore you, lay our lives before you. How we love you.
> Jesus we adore you, lay our lives before you. How we love you.
> Spirit we adore you, lay our lives before you. How we love you."

This can be a reminder that we have been learning about the Father, Son and Holy Spirit in the last three sessions, and that, in church, we often make the sign of the cross with all of their names. You might also talk about how from the beginning of Christianity, people have been building beautiful churches, holy places, where people can meet and worship.

The religious dimension
(in the special place where Jesus speaks to us)

Lighting the candle

Include a chalice and paten on the focal point. If you are using the altar as your focal point, use one of the altar candles. You might encourage people to think about how we light the candles on the altar during Mass. It helps us remember that Jesus is present during Mass, just as he is present with us now.

Greeting the scripture

You might use a hymn called "The Lord is in His Holy Temple" taken directly from Habakkuk (a seventh century prophet). The words are perfect for this session:

> "The Lord is in his holy temple; let all the earth keep silence before him ×2"

Sign our heads, mouths and hearts

Remind people why we sign our heads, our mouths and our hearts.

Note:

Be aware that, in some circumstances, there are medical or other reasons why the church cannot be the special place in this session. If this is the case, the session can still introduce the idea of special places where people meet to pray by using photos, power-points and tableaux. Special or sacred items can still be made available to people to explore if this happens.

Listening to Jesus in the scripture

Holding the book, read the scripture clearly and reverently to the whole group using an adapted version of the Gospel of John 2:14-16

> Jesus went up to Jerusalem. Inside the temple,
> he saw people selling cattle and sheep and pigeons.
> And there were others changing money for people.
> Jesus said: "Take all this out of here
> And stop turning my Father's house into a market."
> Then he chased the cattle and the sheep out of the temple.
> He knocked over the money tables and their coins fell on the ground.
> He said: "God's house is not a market; it is a place of prayer."

Giving the scripture message to each person

Now approach each member of the group individually, holding their hands and looking into their eyes, saying, "[name] Jesus tells you today:

> God's house is a special place; God's house is a place of prayer."

Reading the scripture again to the whole group

After each person has heard Jesus speaking to them, the message is then given to the whole group again.

Breaking the scripture open

We suggest that you invite people to approach the focal point and to look closely at the sacred vessels, the candles, the holy book and touch them carefully if they want to. As they do this, you might sing Bob Gillman's hymn:

> "Bind us together, Lord, Bind us together with cords that cannot be broken.
> Bind us together, Lord, bind us together, Bind us together with love."

This will give the message that we come together as one family, brothers and sisters with Christ, all together in God's house. Say we will find all these things in every Catholic church we go into. Depending on your group, and whether they come from different parishes, they may comment on how they all find these things in their churches.

Note:

For people who have difficulty in listening to a long Gospel, use only the first four lines and the last line of this scripture, or consider accompanying the reading of the Gospel with signing.

Alternatively:
An idea to add to the singing of "Bind us together" is to replace the verses with a holding hands activity which joins all the group together as the body of Christ. Simply replace the verses with names in the following way: "Jane can hold hands with Laura and Laura can hold hands with Katie, Katie can hold hands with Freddie and Freddie can hold hands with Sean," then back to the chorus, repeat until everybody is joined.

Getting the message

Help people make the link between how they prepare for visitors at home and the special things they use, and how they have seen and touched all the special things we have in church for when we celebrate Mass. Give people time to hear Jesus is saying that to them today. You might sing or listen to the hymn "Be still" while they listen to him. You might bring this part of the session to a close with some quiet prayer. Invite the participants to say their own prayer if they want. Here is an idea:

> "Thank you, Jesus, for bringing us together in this special place.
> Help us to make this a place where we turn to you and always find you here with us. Amen."

Sharing the message/celebrate

It's time to celebrate; to share what it was like to learn about the church as a building. They may want to celebrate the fact that, from the beginning of Christianity, people wanted to build beautiful churches where they could meet and worship God. They may be excited that they were allowed to be in the church, to move around more freely than usual and to touch things they've never touched before. They may want to say what they liked the most. If your activity has used a toy church or images that have been cut out, you might invite people to choose one item they especially liked. You might encourage them to tell the group why they chose that item. They may be looking forward to coming to Mass on Sunday so that they can tell their families what they learned today. Remember: this sharing is important; it is helping to build friendships in the group.

 Remember, for this session, you will need:

 To introduce the session:
Pictures of churches, especially the parishes of those in the group.

 Activity and special place (which may be the church):
- Crayons, paints and papers if you are drawing the images of the inside of the church.
- If you choose to use the picture puzzle in the activity book from the CD, you may need scissors and glue; or, if you are providing the cut outs, you will have to prepare them in advance and you will need laser card and Velcro.
- You will need to ask if you can use:
  a chalice, ciborium, a procession cross, a candle on a candle stand (possibly the paschal candle) and altar missal.

 You will also need, as always:
- the holy book with the simplified reading placed inside, an icon of Christ, draped cloth and your candle, (unless you are going to light the paschal candle).
Music (all of which can be found on YouTube):
- Bob Gillman, "Bind us together".
- Terry Coelho's, "Father we adore you". You can buy an MP3 copy, and sheet music on www.audiblefaith.com/pages/sg853003.
- W.H. McAllister, "The Lord is in His Holy Temple" taken directly from Habakkuk.
- David J. Evans', "Be still, for the presence of the Lord" - verse one.

5. We are the Body of Christ

 Session aim To learn how each member of the Christian community is needed, and each of us has a part to play.

Preparing for the session

In the last session, we learned about sacred items in the church. In this session, we will be looking at the people in the church, and how we all make up the Body of Christ. When we watched the Olympics and the Paralympics in the summer of 2012, we knew many of the athletes by name. We knew what part they were playing and how well they were doing. Each member of the team was needed; each had an important part to play.

In a similar way, our parishes are the same and every member of the community has a part to play. Ask the participants if they belong to any teams or groups and ask them about all the different people on the team. Alternatively, you can ask them about the different members of their family and the various jobs each of them has in the house (cleaning, cooking, setting the table, earning money to pay the bills, and so on.). People are likely to enjoy sharing experiences; the conversation will give others ideas and it will open the session up.

Paul's first letter to the Corinthians 12:12-17. 20

¹² *Just as a body has many members*
and all the members of the body,
though many, are one body, so it is with Christ.
¹³ *For in the one Spirit we were all baptised*
into one body — Jews or Greeks, slaves or free —
and we were all made to drink of one Spirit.
¹⁴ *Indeed the body does not consist*
of one member but of many.
¹⁵ *If the foot would say: "I am not a hand,*
so I do not belong to the body"
that would not make it any less a part of the body.
¹⁶ *And if the ear would say: "I am not an eye,*
so I do not belong to the body"

that would not make it any less a part of the body.
[17] *If the whole body were an eye,*
where would the sense of smell be?
[20] *As it is, there are many members, yet one body."*

In this session, we are looking at how one of the main purposes of the church is service. We will be focusing on how each of us has a part to play in serving others. In other words, each of us has a ministry and there are many different ministries.

Invite some members of the parish who are involved in various ministries to come and share something about what they do. We suggest that you prepare the visitors well. Explain that you will introduce them at the beginning but invite them to speak about their ministries only when the group is breaking open the scripture. Warn them that the participants may have a very short attention span, so they may keep their talk to only a sentence or two. For example, the flower arranger may simply say that s/he makes beautiful flower arrangements to worship God and to make the church a beautiful place for people who come to pray. She might finish by saying: "What would it be like if there were no flowers?"

By way of preparing yourself for this session, think of all the ministries you can name in your parish and thank God for them. You might also think of things that the participants can do in the parish.

The Catechism

The Catechism tells us that baptism makes us members of the Body of Christ; it incorporates us into the Church. From the baptismal font is born the one People of God "for by one Spirit we were all baptised into one body" (1 Cor 12:13; CCC 1267).

Leading the session

Welcome

Every session begins with the welcome of each person by name. In this session, say we will be hearing about how each member of the parish is needed. Each and every one of us has a part to play.

The human dimension
(the activity drawing on our life experience)

In this session, I suggest that you make a fruit salad. Give each person a different job. The fruit salad will be delicious only if everyone does his/her job.

- Get some of the people to prepare different fruits for the salad. Some may cut apples; others may peel bananas and cut them up; others might peel a tangerine and break it into segments for the salad.
- Someone can find a bowl to put the salad into; some can set the table.
- Someone will want to set out small bowls to serve the salad in at the end of the session.

By getting people to do different jobs using lots of fruits for one fruit salad, we can gently lead people into the concept that the Christian community is made up of many different people and they all make up the Body of Christ. In this session, we are going to make a fruit salad.

David Tunnell helping to make a fruit salad in his group

From here, we move to our special place. Invite people to bring the fruit salad and add it to the focal point. This will help people to link their life experience with their faith experience. As people enter the special place, you might have some quiet music with quiet words. I suggest that you use something familiar and appropriate. For example, David Evans' "Be still for the presence of the Lord. The holy one is here".

The religious dimension
(in the special place where Jesus speaks to us)

Lighting the candle

We light the candle to remind us that Jesus is the light in our lives and he is here with us. Remember, this is the signal that a new phase of the session is beginning and it helps to shift the mood and help people enter into the religious experience.

Greeting the scripture

Consider using one of Christopher Walker's acclamations: the Salisbury one or the Celtic one (which was written with Fintan O'Carroll).

Sign our heads, mouths and hearts

Remind people that we sign our heads because we hear God's word, our hearts because we proclaim it with our mouths and we feel it in our hearts.

Listening to Jesus in the scripture

Holding the book, read the scripture clearly and reverently to the whole group using an adapted version of St Paul's first letter to the 1 Corinthians 12:12-20

> Different parts of our bodies have different jobs to do.
> Each part is different; each is important.
> A body needs all the parts to work together.
> You need a head to think, eyes to see, hands to hold,
> feet to walk, ears to hear.
> If your whole body was just an eye,
> how would you hear anything?
> If your whole body was just an ear,
> how would you smell anything?
> All these parts make up one body.

Giving the scripture message to each person

Now approach each member of the group individually, holding their hands and looking into their eyes, saying,

> "[Name] Jesus tells us today that
> all of us together make up the Body of Christ;
> and each of us has a part to play."

Reading the scripture again to the whole group

After each person has heard Jesus speaking to them, the message is then given to the whole group again.

Breaking the scripture open

Introduce the visiting ministers again. This time, tell the group what each of them does in the parish. Then invite them to say something brief about their ministries. Pause afterwards and ask the participants what they do in the parish, or what they would like to do. Ask them if they can see why they made a fruit salad at the beginning of the session.

Getting the message

Sometimes, people with learning disabilities are not included in the many jobs there are to do in the parish. The idea that God calls each and every one of us and asks us to do some service in the parish may come as a surprise to them. Give people time to hear that Jesus is saying they do have a part to play. For example, you would miss the oranges if we took them out of the fruit salad. In the same way, the parish is not the same if anyone is missing, if anyone does not play their part.

Note:

If it is not possible to get visitors in for this session, you might consider using a PowerPoint or downloaded images or objects related to the different ministries to engage with different levels of ability.
See also a text resource in the *I Call You Friends* pack downloadable for a small fee from their website (http://www.widgit.com/resources/curriculum/re/i_call_you_friends/index.htm).

© The Tunnell family

Close this part of the session

Bring this part of the session to a close with a hymn, for example: "My God loves me".

"My God loves me; His love will never end.
He rests within my heart for my God loves me."

You are now ready to move to the place where you will celebrate.

Sharing the message/celebrating

I suspect that it will not be difficult for people to share at the end of this session. Eat the fruit salad that was made at the beginning of the session for the celebration and remind people how each piece of fruit, though different, is important for the salad to be what it is. Friendships will have now begun to form and people will be aware of the gifts of one another. Just as they can appreciate the different pieces of fruit, invite them to appreciate and celebrate the gifts of one another, the things without which this group would not be the same. You might begin the celebration with a blessing: "We thank you Jesus, for the gift of today, for the gift of this time together. We thank you for the fruit, for the visitors, but mostly, we thank you for the gift of one another and the friendships you are giving us."

 Remember, for this session, you will need

 To introduce the session:
Photos of teams. If possible, have pictures of the Paralympics in the summer of 2012, which can be found on the internet.

 Activity and special place:
- People in the parish involved in ministries, or a PowerPoint or images to show the various ministries in the parish. You will also need a selection of seasonal fruits for the salad, apples, bananas, tangerines, a large bowl, some small bowls, spoons, a tablecloth and table decorations.
- You will need, as always: the holy book with the simplified reading placed inside, draped cloth, a candle, an icon of Christ or a crucifix.

Music:
- Christopher Walker's acclamations: the Salisbury one or the Celtic one (written with Fintan O'Carroll).
- David Evans' "Be still for the presence of the Lord; the holy one is here".
- "My God loves me" first verse, Anonymous. See the free download of sheet music: http://www.scribd.com/doc/29808879/My-God-Loves-me.
- Bob Gillman's, "Bind us together" which includes the words "there is only one body" in the verse.

Celebration:

The first step on the journey

Accepting the invitation to follow Jesus

Celebration: a rite accepting the invitation to follow Jesus, and a rite of welcome

 Session aim To learn how each member of the Christian community is needed; each of us has a part to play.

Preparing for the session

By this point, people will hopefully have begun to want to belong to the Church; they will want to know Jesus, or to know him better. This celebration (or step, on our journey of faith) is an important stopping point. For those who are already baptised, it offers the opportunity for them to say: "Yes, I accept Jesus' invitation to know him better, to follow him more closely." For those who are not yet baptised and who are preparing to be baptised, it is an opportunity for them to say: "Yes, I accept Jesus' invitation to know him and to be part of his Church."

Read Matthew 4:18-22

¹⁸ *As Jesus walked by the Sea of Galilee, he saw two brothers*
   Simon, who is called Peter, and Andrew his brother
   who were casting a net into the sea — for they were fishermen.
¹⁹ *And he said to them:*
   "Follow me and I will make you fish for people."
²⁰ *Immediately they left their nets and followed him.*
²¹ *As they went from there, he saw two other brothers,*
   James son of Zebedee and his brother John
   in the front of the boat with their father Zebedee,
   mending their nets and he called them.
²² *Immediately they left the boat and their father*
   and followed him.

Read the Gospel of Matthew and reflect on what it must have been like for the disciples to be invited by Jesus to follow him.

Previous page:
Duccio di Buoninsegna,
Calling of Peter and Andrew,
c. 1310
(National Gallery of Art,
Washington, D.C.)

The rite

This rite is the first step towards baptism; but it can also be adapted to be a rite of welcome for those who are already baptised and who are preparing to become Catholic. Or, it can be a rite for the baptised people to formally accept Jesus' invitation to know him better. The rite suggests that a small group of people be present to celebrate this step, members of the faith community, parents or guardians, will probably be there (RCIA 250). The celebration can take place in the church or in the special place if people will be more comfortable there (RCIA 251).

In this first ritual celebration, we reflect on the significance of being "marked" as followers of Jesus. People have already spent some time in session 2 learning how, in baptism, we are marked with the sign of the cross to show that we belong to Jesus. In this rite, people are signed on all their senses (RCIA 266):

- the head as a reminder of how much Jesus loves us;
- the ears to help us to hear and listen to his words;
- the eyes to help us see the works of God;
- the lips to help us speak as Jesus would speak;
- the heart to help make it a home for Jesus;
- the shoulders to help us be strong, like Jesus;
- the hands to help us touch others with Jesus' gentleness;
- the feet to help us walk in the way of Jesus.

By way of preparing yourself for the rite, consider how powerful this rite will be for people. Think about how often you remember how much Jesus loves you, how well you allow Jesus to use your senses for his work in the world.

Leading the liturgy

Welcome

As always, every session begins with the welcome of each person by name. In this liturgy, you might say: "Jesus will be inviting us to follow him. We will be having a celebration! Will you accept his invitation?"

The RCIA (the Rite of Christian Initiation of Adults) is the way people become Christians in the Catholic Church. Part II of the RCIA, Rites for Particular Circumstances, allows us to adapt the rite for people in exceptional circumstances in which the process of Christian initiation is not followed in its complete form.

Note

Consider the idea of preparing a booklet for this liturgy using symbol supported text to assist with engagement and participation if possible. Also consider, signing one another on all your senses if you are preparing this session with others, using the words from the adaptation of the rite on p. 82. Spend some time reflecting on how you allow Jesus to use your senses for his work in the world.

The human dimension
(the activity drawing on our life experience)

Ask people to think about times when they have been welcomed somewhere they feel they belong. Perhaps it was:

- at a new school
- to a football team
- at a friend's house
- in your parish.

Ask them what helped them feel they belonged:

- Was it their school uniform or their football kit?
- Was it that they were part of a group all doing the same thing?

Ask if the uniform or the kit they wear "mark" them to show that they belong:
Ask what it is like to feel that you belong, to be welcomed.
Ask if they are the one who welcomes others.

The religious dimension
(in the special place where Jesus speaks to us)

Moving to the special place

Invite everyone to move to the special place: the church or your usual special place if you think they will be more comfortable there. Using the oil of catechumens is another way of engaging the senses. The scent will remain as a reminder that Jesus has invited them. [This part of the rite is optional, though, and you may decide not to use it. It is only for the unbaptised; and note that, if you do use it, the minister has to be a priest or a deacon.]

As you move from one place to the other, you might sing or listen to the chorus of "Will you come and follow me if I but call your name". (Note: you may want to adapt some of the words, especially for autistic people, who can take what we say literally and may become upset at some of the words.)

Lighting the candle

As always, light the candle as a sign that the celebration is about to begin and Jesus is present with us.

Greeting the Gospel

Since this is a special celebration, you might use the "Halle, halle, halle" acclamation. It is Traditional Caribbean, easy to learn and very joyful.

Sign our heads, mouths and hearts

Remind people why we sign our heads, our mouths and our hearts as we prepare to listen to God's word.

Listening to Jesus in the scripture

Holding the book, read the scripture clearly and reverently to the whole group using an adapted version of Matthew 4:18-22

> As Jesus walked by the Sea of Galilee,
> he saw two brothers Simon, called Peter, and
> Andrew his brother who were fishing.
> And he said to them: "Follow me"
> Immediately they left their nets and followed him.
> As they went from there, he saw two other brothers,
> James son of Zebedee and his brother John
> in the front of the boat with their father Zebedee,
> mending their nets and he called them too.
> Immediately they left the boat and their father and followed him.

Giving the scripture message to each person

Now approach each member of the group individually, holding their hands and looking into their eyes, saying:

> "[Name] Jesus says to you today: Will you come and follow me if I call you?"

Reading the scripture again to the whole group

After each person has heard Jesus speaking to them, the message is then given to the whole group again.

Note:

For people who have difficulty in listening to a long Gospel, use only the first five lines of this scripture.

Note:

An alternative for breaking open the scripture in this session which engages children with learning disabilities and through which they can affirm their intention to follow Jesus, is either in word, sign, eye-contact or gesture. "Do you want to follow Jesus x 3 and be his special friend? Yes, I want to follow Jesus and be his special friend." (Sung to the tune of "What shall we do with the drunken sailor".) This works well when used alongside animation of the gospel using toy magnetic fishing rods and fish and other enjoyable sensory toys and materials associated with the seaside location of the gospel story.

Breaking the scripture open

Invite people to play the game, "Simon says". Make sure to include these actions:

- Simon says: "Come and follow me" as he invites the others to follow him around the room where you are meeting.
- Simon says: "Stop! Touch your head."
- Simon says: "Now, touch your mouth."
- Simon says: "Touch your ear; then the other one."
- Simon says: "Follow me some more."
- Simon says: "Stop! Touch your heart."
- Simon says: "Touch your hand; then the other one."
- Simon says: "Now, reach down and touch your feet."
- Simon says: "Follow me some more around the special place."
- Then, Simon says: "Go back to your place."

Ask people if they enjoyed doing what Simon told them to do. Jesus is asking them to follow him. Ask them if they will follow him.

The rite of signing

Find a way to explain what the signing means. For some, you might explain it before the priest does it; for others, it may be more effective for the priest to explain it as he does it. Use this text or adapt it:

Priest: The cross is a sign of being a follower of Jesus. I will mark your forehead with a cross. Jesus is inviting you to be his friend. He wants you to remember him always.

Priest: Think about the kind of things you listen to. Jesus wants you to hear him and to listen to him so I will mark your ears.

Priest: Think about the things you do with your eyes. Do you see and appreciate the beautiful world God has created for us? Do you see the people who love you? I will mark your eyes with the sign of the cross. Jesus wants you to see the works of God.

Priest: Now think about how you use your lips to speak and the kind of things you say. Are you kind? Can people tell that you are a follower of Jesus by the things you say to them? I will mark your lips so that you can accept the invitation to speak like Jesus.

Priest: I will mark your heart with the sign of the cross, making it a home for Jesus. Jesus wants you to love him and to love yourself.

Priest: I will mark your shoulders with the sign of the cross, so that you will be strong; to make you strong like Jesus.

Priest: I will mark your hands with the sign of the cross. Jesus invites you to touch yourself and others with his gentleness.

Priest: And, last, I will mark your feet with the sign of the cross. Jesus invites you to know him better, to follow him more closely.

After the signing, ask the question: "Will you accept Jesus' invitation to know him better; to follow him more closely?" When they reply "Yes," you might present each person with the gift of a simple wooden cross.

The rite finishes with this beautiful prayer over you. Listen to the words as your catechist or your priest reads it:

> "Lord, you have filled these people with the desire to become perfect Christians. As they grow in wisdom and knowledge, respond to their hopes and answer their prayers. We ask this through Christ, our Lord, Amen."

Sharing the message

Your celebration after this rite should be a little more special than usual. Let people know how happy you are that they have accepted Jesus' invitation. Make sure family, friends and this faith community tell people how special it is that they are telling the world that they want to follow Jesus. They will tell others they are followers of Jesus when they wear their cross and when they love others as they love themselves.

 Remember, for this session, you will need:

To invite the priest to do the signing and close family members and friends;

 To introduce the session:

School uniform, football kit, and so on: things that show belonging to groups.

 Activity and special place (which may be the church):

- You will need the oil of catechumens for the anointings (optional).
- If you decide to give wooden crosses to people, you will need to buy them. They are easily available on the internet.
- You will need, as always: the holy book with the simplified reading placed inside, an icon of Christ and a draped cloth and your candle.
- If you decide to use the alternative fishing activity, you will need the magnetic fishing rods and fish and other sensory toys and materials associated with the seaside location of the Gospel story.

 Music:

- "The Summons", or "Will you come and follow Me". Words, John L Bell and Graham Maule, Iona or "Follow me, follow me" (music by Sr Madeleine and words by Michael Cockett).
- "Halle, halle, halle" Gospel acclamation, traditional Caribbean, arr. John Bell.

Confirming and strengthening baptism in the sacrament of confirmation

6. My Spirit will help you

 Session aim To see how God has sent the Holy Spirit to help us and to remind us of Jesus' teachings.

Preparing for the session

In this session, we are reminded that Jesus promised that although he would not be here in person with us, he would not leave us on our own, he would send the Spirit to help us (John 14:25). Over two thousand years later, we continue to believe in this promise. There are times when we simply know that the Spirit is with us.

This is the first of three sessions which can be used to prepare people for the sacrament of confirmation. Those who are already baptised may be preparing to be confirmed; those who are not yet baptised may be preparing for all three sacraments.

John 14:23-26

23 *Jesus told the disciples:*
"Those who love me will keep my word,
and my Father will love them, and we will come to them
and make our home with them.
24 *Whoever does not love me does not keep my words;*
and the word that you hear is not mine,
but is from the Father who sent me.
25 *"I have said these things to you while I am still with you.*
26 *But the Advocate, the Holy Spirit,*
whom the Father will send in my name,
will teach you everything,
and remind you of all that I have said to you."

This Gospel is part of St John's discourse on the Holy Spirit. Jesus is reassuring his disciples that, although he will no longer be physically present among them, they will experience his presence in a new way by continuing to love him and by living according to his commandments.

In addition, he and the Father would send another who would be a supporting Advocate, or Paraclete, to remain among them. It is that same Holy Spirit that continues to inspire us to do good things today. We cannot see the Spirit, but the Holy Spirit, the Spirit of Jesus, is in us and helps us.

The Catechism

On the day of Pentecost, the Spirit of the Promise was poured out on the disciples, who were gathered "together in one place" (Acts 2:1). While awaiting the Spirit, "all these with one accord devoted themselves to prayer" (Acts 1:14). It is the Spirit who teaches the Church and recalls for her everything that Jesus said (John 14:26) (CCC 2623).

The Church's prayer is founded on the faith of the apostles; it is authenticated by charity and is nourished in the Eucharist (CCC 2624). The Holy Spirit keeps the memory of Christ alive in his Church at prayer (CCC 2625).

By way of preparing yourself for this session, think about the times when you have experienced the desire to do a random act of kindness; or if someone else has been unexpectedly kind to you and helped you when they didn't have to. It may be that you saw an elderly person or a small child who needs help. You might say, of course, anyone would help them.

Leading the session

Welcome

As always, the session begins with the welcome of each person by name. In this session, we are reminded of Jesus' promise that, although he would not be here in person with us, he would not leave us on our own, he would send the Spirit to help us.

The human dimension
(the activity drawing on our life experience)

The activity I suggest for this session is to make a poster called "helping hands" to make the link between the gifts God has given us and how we use them to help others.

Using a piece of lining paper and finger paints, invite people to put a handprint on the paper.

While they do that, they can share with one another times when they have offered a helping hand to others. Ask them if they think God's Spirit was there, encouraging them to be kind, loving, helpful, and so on. The poster is the symbol you will bring to your special place.

Moving to the special place

Get as many people as possible to carry the poster to the special place and hang it up so that everyone can see it.

The religious dimension
(in the special place where Jesus speaks to us)

Lighting the candle

We light the candle to remind us that Jesus is the light in our lives and he is here with us encouraging us, guiding us and helping us.

Greeting the scripture

You might consider singing Daniel Iverson's,

> "Spirit of the living God, fall afresh on me,
> Spirit of the living God, fall afresh on me.
> Break me, melt me, mould me, fill me.
> Spirit of the living God, fall afresh on me."

It is very appropriate for this session and it was used earlier in these materials, so people may remember it.

Sign our heads, mouths and hearts

Remind people we do this because we hear God's word in our heads, proclaim it with our mouths and feel it in our hearts.

Listening to Jesus in the scripture

Holding the book, speak reverently and clearly and read the scripture to the whole group. We suggest using this adapted version of the Gospel of John 14:23-26.

Making the helping hands poster

Jesus told the disciples,

> "Those who love me will obey my words, and, as I have said,
> my Father will love them — and he is the one who sent me.
> I am telling you this while I am still here
> but my Father will send you the Holy Spirit
> who will teach you everything you need to know
> and will remind you of everything I taught you."

Giving the scripture message to each person

Now approach each member of the group individually, saying,

> "[Name], Jesus says to you today:
> The Holy Spirit will teach you everything you need to know and will remind you
> to help others as I taught you."

Reading the scripture again to the whole group

After each person has heard Jesus speaking to them, the message is then given to the whole group.

Breaking the scripture open

The activity was about how our hands are "helping hands". Listen to the words of Carey Landry's "Holy hands" and consider playing the first part of it:

"These are holy hands. God's given us holy hands.
God works through our hands and so our hands are holy. These are holy hands. God's given us holy hands.
God works through our hands and so our hands are holy. God is present here and so has crowned us holy."

The Holy Spirit inspires us to do good things; to offer helping hands to those we live with and those we meet. When we offer helping hands, our hands are holy hands. The Holy Spirit will help us any time we ask for help. Jesus promised that the Holy Spirit would always be with us and Jesus keeps his promises.

Getting the message

Explain that some people describe the Holy Spirit as fire or wind or as a dove. Using blowing bubbles and a gentle fan may help them feel the Spirit. You might sing "Spirit of the Living God, fall afresh on [name]" — going around the room and including the name of each person as you blow the bubbles over them. Pause afterwards to give people time to hear what Jesus is saying that to them today.

Sharing the message/celebrating

It's time to celebrate; to share the Good News with one another. Hopefully, people will have enjoyed their finger painting activity, the bubbles, the wind, and so on. and they will be feeling full of the Holy Spirit! You might give them each a bottle of bubbles to use during the celebration and suggest they take it home afterwards as a memento of the session.

Remember how important it is for people to enjoy this part of the session with the friends they have made during these sessions. By now, they are beginning to know one another better and to trust one another. They may be meeting one another in between sessions and enlarging their circle of support. You might ask people to say how they have changed since theses sessions began. Are they more like Jesus? Are they more loving and more caring? Do they share more easily and are they kinder to others? Are they doing good things with their holy hands?

✓ **Remember, for this session, you'll need:**

✓ **To introduce the session:**
Ideas of how people are helpful.

✓ **Activity and special place:**
 • Lining paper and finger paints. an orange/red cloth. You will also need, as always: the holy book with the simplified reading placed inside a crucifix.
 • An icon of Pentecost, a candle.
 • Blowing bubbles and an electric fan.

✓ **Music:** • Find versions of both on YouTube.
 • Daniel Iverson's "Spirit of the living God".
 • "Holy hands" by Carey Landry (*A day in the life*: Chaplain Carey Landry).

7. The gifts of the Holy Spirit

Session aim To introduce the concept of thinking about what Jesus would do — and choosing to do what Jesus would do.

Preparing for the session

Everyone wants to love and to be loved; it's what we all have in common. St Paul said that the best of all the gifts is love. In this session, we will look at the gifts of the Spirit and how, in love, all the gifts come together.

Love is an abstract concept, so you need to find concrete examples to share with people. In the photo below, a boy is holding a young puppy; it's going to be his dog and he's been promised that he will be the one who takes care of the puppy, feeds him, walks him, and so on. His parents are giving him an opportunity: they are giving him the chance to love something and to learn how to care for it. Think of how many gifts the boy will discover as he learns just how much love he can give and receive from this puppy.

In this session and in the next one, we will be exploring the gifts of the Holy Spirit. We can begin by looking at what the gifts of the Spirit can do for the boy and his puppy. The gift of wisdom, which is more about attitude than it is about how old we are or how much we know. It will help the boy use his gifts to their fullest potential. In time, the boy will hopefully become aware that these gifts come from God.

Photo: Diana Klein

The boy will use right judgement when he makes the loving and responsible choices he will be faced with in caring for his puppy. The gift of courage will help him use his gifts to love the puppy without the fear of failing; he will instinctively know that what is most important is the love they have for one another.

The gift of understanding will lead him to believe that God cares about each of us in the same way as he cares about the puppy. The gift of this knowledge is about coming to know that this is what God is like.

The gift of reverence develops as respect develops. It helps us to treat all God's creatures with dignity and to be aware that we are loving a human or an animal who is also loved unconditionally by God. The gift of wonder and awe is about being increasingly conscious of the love of God.

Read St Paul's first letter to the Corinthians 12:4-11

4 *Now there are varieties of gifts, but the same spirit;*
5 *and there are varieties of services, but the same Lord*
6 *and there are varieties of activities but it is the same God*
   who activates all of them in everyone.
7 *To each is given the manifestation of the Spirit for the common good.*
8 *To one is given through the Spirit the utterance of wisdom,*
   and to another the utterance of knowledge according to the same Spirit.
9 *to another faith by the same Spirit,*
   to another gifts of healing by one Spirit,
10 *to another the working of miracles, to another prophecy,*
   to another the discernment of spirits, to another various kinds of tongues,
   to another the interpretation of tongues.
11 *All these are activated by one and the same Spirit*
   who allots to each one individually just as the Spirit chooses.

This letter goes on to talk about how we are all members of the Body of Christ and how we need one another. If anyone of any age or ability is missing from the Body of Christ, his Body is incomplete; each of us is, in fact, indispensable. A little later in that first letter to the Corinthians, St Paul says: "The members of the body that seem to be weaker are indispensable" (1 Corinthians 12:22). Notice that St Paul says, "they seem to be weaker". He understands this misperception and in contrast more their indispensability. We must ensure the rightful place of all people in the heart of the believing community.

Reflect:

You are invited to think about what gifts you have; how you would describe yourself. If you have a problem thinking about your gifts, ask those you live with and work with; ask your friends. It is a good exercise! Then thank God for all the gifts you have been given.

The Catechism

The Catechism reminds us that God, who created humans out of love also calls them to love; the fundamental and innate vocation of every human being. For we are created in the image and likeness of God, who is himself love (Genesis 1:27) (CCC 1604). With the gifts God gives to us, this love which God blesses can be used for the service of others.

Remember too, that "God is love and in himself he lives a mystery of personal loving communion. Creating the human race in his own image . . . God inscribed in the humanity of man and woman the vocation, and thus the capacity and responsibility, of love and communion" (CCC 2331).

By way of preparing yourself for this session, you might take some time to think about your vocation and your capacity and responsibilities of love. You might think, too, and thank God for the gifts you have been given. Reflect on the many different ways you use the gifts God has given you to be a loving person and try to be more conscious of God's presence in your life.

Leading the session

Welcome

As always, the session begins with the welcome of each person by name. In this session, you might say: "Jesus welcomes you today [name]. He is here with us to assure us that the gifts of the Holy Spirit help us find ways of being loving."

The human dimension
(the activity drawing on our life experience)

In this session, we will use Widgit cards to answer the questions: "What gifts do we have?" and "What are we good at?" The idea is to acknowledge our gifts, which have come from God, and to say we are willing to offer them back to God in the service of others. Have a beautifully wrapped gift box with ribbon and a bow on it and a slot on the top which will fit lotto cards. Then offer the group a selection of lotto cards and ask them to choose which gifts they have — inviting them to put them in the slot. Make sure you have plenty of duplicates. Ask the participants how would they describe themselves? They may say:

I am helpful

I am patient

I share

Good listener

I am kind

I care

Or, what are they good at?

I am good at making things

I am good at drawing

I am good at singing

I am fun to be with

I am good at dancing

I am good at sports

To support these sessions, ICYF Pack 2 has confirmation lotto and gifts and fruit lotto (available for a small fee from the Widgit website (http://www.widgit.com/resources/curriculum/re/i_call_you_friends/index.htm).

Moving to the special place

The symbol you will carry to the special place is the box with everyone's gifts, which should be carried carefully to the special place.

The religious dimension
(in the special place where Jesus speaks to us)

Lighting the candle

We light the candle to remind us that Jesus is the light in our lives and he is here with us.

Greeting the scripture

You might use Linda Stassen's "Sing Alleluia to the Lord" as your Gospel acclamation in this session.

Sign our heads, mouths and hearts

If you think people might like a variation on explaining what you are doing, you might make this into a prayer:

> "Lord, help us to hear God's word in our heads,
> to proclaim it with our mouths and to feel it in our hearts."

Listening to Jesus in the scripture

Holding the book, speak reverently and clearly and read the scripture to the whole group. We suggest using this (or another) simplified version of the letter of St Paul to the Corinthians, 1 Cor 12:4-11

> There are many gifts, but the same Spirit;
> and there are many services, but the same Lord
> and there are many activities but the same God
> gives all of them to everyone.
> Each person is given the gifts of the Spirit for the common good.
> One person is given wisdom, another is given knowledge,
> another is given faith and yet another
> the gift of helping others and telling them what God wants.
> All these are given by one and the same
> Spirit who gives the gifts to each one of us just as the Spirit chooses.

Giving the scripture message to each person

Now approach each member of the group individually, saying:

> "[Name] Jesus says to you today:
> Now there are many gifts, but it is the same Holy Spirit who gives them all."

Reading the scripture again to the whole group

After each person has heard Jesus speaking to them, the message is then given to the whole group.

Breaking the scripture open

Wrap a candle for each person in the group and place all of them into a box beautifully wrapped. Place the box on the focal point during the reading of the scripture. You might consider tea-light battery candles or prayer cards with a picture of a candle on them for safety reasons depending on your participants. Then ask: "How many of you like getting presents?" and "How many of you like to give presents?" Tell the group that today we are going to talk about a present we get that will remind us of the Holy Spirit, and that we will share with others in a special way.

Get someone to open the box and distribute the gifts of candles. Then, ask everyone to unwrap their candle gift. Invite one person to go to the candle on the focal point to light their candle (with a long match or a taper). Then share the light on that candle with the other people one by one (if it is safe to do so). The one light (symbolic of the Holy Spirit) has given its light to everyone. It has not diminished in its power by sharing its light and now everyone has a lighted candle. God says in the scripture we heard that the Holy Spirit gives us gifts that are not only for us, but also for those around us.

Getting the message

Give people time to hear Jesus is saying that to them today. Be aware that the scripture message and what people hear Jesus saying may not be one and the same. You might play "Share the light of Jesus" by Bernadette Farrell. It is a really good one for signing and accompanying with percussion and would mediate the message of this session well.

Sharing the message/celebrating

It's time to celebrate, to share the Good News with one another. It is time to have refreshments where people can share with one another what they have learned about their gifts and the gifts of the others in the group.

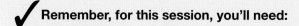 **Remember, for this session, you'll need:**

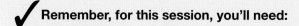 **To introduce the session:**
A story about how we use the gifts we have (such as the one I told about the boy and his puppy).

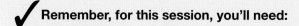 **Activity and special place:**
A wrapped gift box with a slot in the top, a selection of lotto cards with Widgit symbols on them, a candle in a wrapped box for each participant. You will also need, as always: the holy book with the simplified reading placed inside, draped cloth, a candle, icon or crucifix.

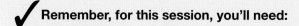 **Music:**
• Linda Stassen's "Sing alleluia to the Lord". There are a number of versions of this on YouTube; it is not something you need accompaniment with.
• Bernadette Farrell's "Share the Light". The "Share the Light" CD includes American and British Sign Language.

8. Being anointed

Session aim

We are anointed with holy oil as priests, prophets and kings are anointed.
We are given the Gifts of the Spirit to do God's work.

Preparing for the session

In this session, we continue to prepare to be confirmed. We will hear how we are anointed with holy oil to give us the strength we need to do God's will. You might remember seeing the coronation of Queen Elizabeth at Westminster Abbey. (It is shown from time to time; most recently for the anniversary of the coronation.)

In the bible, kings in the Old Testament were anointed with oil. Did you know that a British coronation is a religious service? The anointing signifies the blessing of the Holy Spirit, just as it does in the sacrament of confirmation. The queen sat in King Edward's chair and the archbishop anointed her in the form of a cross on the palms of both of her hands, saying: "Be thy hands anointed with holy oil." Then, he anointed her on the breast, saying: "Be thy breast anointed with oil." Finally, he anointed her on the crown of her head, saying: "Be thy head anointed with holy oil, as kings, priests and prophets were anointed." At the coronation, the Queen was asked to make promises to serve the British people; the first time she made this promise was when she was a princess. She did so because she was the child of a king and heir to the throne. Likewise, we are children of God and co-heirs with Christ; and this bestows upon us a dignity greater than any earthly monarch can bestow. Our faithfulness, just like the Queen's, springs from our sense of calling, knowing that we have a destiny to fulfil. The knowledge that God has called us to be his children emphasises the relationship we have with

Detail of a miniature of the anointing of the breast of Queen Jeanne from the Coronation Book of Charles V, France (Paris) 1365. Cotton Tiberius B. VIII

96

him. It also shows us that our Father wants us to be Christ-like and bear his image. We are given gifts to use for that purpose. At the coronation, the Queen was commissioned by God to serve her people. We, too, have been commissioned to serve God and one another. To enable us to serve him, God gives us the spiritual gifts that we need. As children of God, we are called to live lives that are faithful to God and his calling upon our lives. We are called to live lives of love towards our fellow human beings, and we are called to love God. Our heavenly Father has anointed us with the Holy Spirit to equip us for this.

Acts of the Apostles 2:1-8. 12-18

1   *When the day of Pentecost had come, they were all together in one place.*
2   *And suddenly from heaven there came a sound like the rush of*
    a violent wind, and it filled the entire house where they were sitting.
3   *Divided tongues, as of fire, appeared among them,*
    and a tongue rested on each of them.
4   *All of them were filled with the Holy Spirit and began*
    to speak in other languages, as the Spirit gave them ability.
5   *Now there were devout Jews from every nation*
    under heaven living in Jerusalem.
6   *And at this sound the crowd gathered and was bewildered,*
    because each one heard them speaking in their native language.
7   *Amazed and astonished, they asked:*
    "Are not all these who are speaking Galileans?
8   *And how is it that we hear, each of us, in our own native language?"*
12 *All were amazed and perplexed, saying to one another:*
    "What does this mean?"
16 *Peter said: "No, this is what was spoken through the prophet Joel:*
17 *'In the last days it will be, God declares, that I will pour out*
    my Spirit upon all flesh and your sons and your daughters shall prophesy,
    and your young men shall see visions, and your old men shall dream dreams.
18 *Even upon my slaves, both men and women, in those days*
    I will pour out my Spirit; and they shall prophesy.'"

The focus of this reading is the mission of the Church: to do God's work with the help of the Holy Spirit. Jesus breathed into his disciples his own life, the Holy Spirit, and by the power of the Holy Spirit, they (and we) are to do what Jesus taught us; to proclaim the great things God has done. Remember that Jesus promised to send his Holy Spirit to give his disciples the power to be his witnesses. In this reading, we see that he has kept his promise.

In our previous sessions, we have talked about the Holy Spirit giving us gifts like wisdom and understanding, and that when the Spirit comes upon us, it feels as gentle as blowing bubbles or like a gentle breeze. In this session's reading, we hear that there was a sound from heaven like the rush of a violent wind; and divided tongues, as of fire, appeared among them, and a tongue rested on each of them. They were all filled with the Holy Spirit and they began to speak in other languages as the Spirit gave them ability.

It is important that people understand that the Holy Spirit is not bubbles or wind or tongues of fire. These are just images to describe something that could not be put into words. It's like describing someone as being as strong as an ox. It is not literal; but similes like these help to understand a feeling or a quality which is abstract.

The Catechism

"Raised from the dead by the glory of the Father" (Romans 6:4), he might immediately give the Holy Spirit by "breathing" on the disciples (cf John 20:22). From this hour onward, the mission of Christ and the Spirit becomes the mission of the Church (CCC 730). Jesus then gave us the "pledge" or "first fruits" of our inheritance: the very life of the Holy Trinity, which is to love "as God [has] loved us" (1 John 4:11-12; cf Romans 8:23; 2 Cor 1:21). This love (the "charity" of 1 Cor 13) is the source of the new life in Christ, made possible because we have received "power" from the Holy Spirit (Acts 1:8; cf 1 Cor 13).

By way of preparing yourself for this session, perhaps you might take some time to think about a time when you were aware of the power you have received from the Holy Spirit.

Leading the session

Welcome

As always, the session begins with the welcome of each person by name, saying something like, "Welcome [name]. It is good to see you today!" In this session, we will hear how we are anointed with holy oil to give us the strength we need to do God's will.

The human dimension
(the activity drawing on our life experience)

In this session, we are going to explore what we use oils and creams for. Invite people to put some of the oil on themselves or on one another if they want to and ask them:

- If they use suntan lotion to protect themselves from the sun;
- If they use antiseptic cream if they have a cut or scrape;
- If athletes use oil on themselves to make themselves stronger;
- If we use bath oil when we are tired and achy;
- If they have ever had a hand or foot massage with aromatherapy oils.

Oils and creams protect, soothe, and refresh us; they strengthen us and they help us with our cooking. Oil is used in religious ceremonies too. The coronation of a king or queen is a religious ceremony and they are anointed with holy oil. Likewise, we are anointed with oil when we are confirmed. The oil is absorbed into us so when we are anointed at our confirmation, God's love, God's Spirit is absorbed into us.

If there is time and if it is possible, you might get people to make crowns or headbands with tongues of fire on them. Otherwise, you might consider making them and giving them to people to help bring the words of scripture come alive. They can then be worn to the special place.

Keep it simple, print out tongues of fire out of red, orange and two tones of yellow. By doubling it over as shown in session 8 of the additional resources CD, you can wrap it around the top of the headband and glue them together.

Moving to the special place
The symbols you will carry to the special place are the oils and lotions you used in the activity.

The religious dimension
(in the special place where Jesus speaks to us)

Lighting the candle

Once people have settled and are quiet, light the candle. The new phase of the session is beginning and we remember Jesus is present with us.

Greeting the scripture

An appropriate hymn for this session might be Daniel Iverson's "Spirit of the living God, fall afresh on me".

Did you know? The oil the Queen was anointed with is kept in a very special vessel called an ampulla: a Latin word for a vessel the Romans used for holding liquids and ointments used to anoint the monarch.

Sign our heads, mouths and hearts

Repeat the variation you used in the last session on explaining what you are doing, you might make this into a prayer:

> "Lord, help us to hear God's word in our heads,
> to proclaim it with our mouths and to feel it in our hearts."

Listening to Jesus in the scripture

Holding the book, speak reverently and clearly and read the scripture to the whole group. Use this simplified version of Acts 2:1-8.

> When the day of Pentecost came they were all together
> in in one place. All of a sudden, they heard a sound like
> a strong wind that seemed to fill the whole house.
> Then they saw what looked like tongues of fire
> coming and resting on each one of them.
> All of them were filled with the Holy Spirit
> and began to speak in other languages.
> At the time, there were visitors from all over the world
> in Jerusalem. They were amazed that they understood
> what the disciples were saying because they were speaking
> in the visitors' languages. They asked how the disciples could
> do that — thinking that the disciples came from Galilee.
> But everyone did understand — the young and the old,
> the rich and the poor, the men and women.

Giving the scripture message to each person

As you give each person the message, I suggest that you turn on a fan and blow wind. Now approach each member of the group individually, holding their hands and looking into their eyes, saying:

> "[Name] Jesus says to you today:
> I send you my Holy Spirit to help you do your job as my follower".

Reading the scripture again to the whole group

After each person has heard Jesus speaking to them, the message is then given to the whole group.

Breaking the scripture open

I suggest that you play Peter Scholes "We are one in the Spirit" during this part of the session. The words lend themselves to asking people to join hands or to using percussion instruments. You might keep a fan blowing gently on people as they sing or listen to the music.

Getting the message

Give people time to hear Jesus is saying that to them today. Be aware that the scripture message and what people hear Jesus saying may not be one and the same.

Sharing the message/celebrating

This is the last of the formation sessions. The remainder of the sessions in these materials are preparations to celebrate the sacraments. By now, people have made friends. It's a good time to stop and celebrate the friendships that have been made; to share what they liked or didn't like about these sessions. It is time to have refreshments with our friends, a time for people talk about the changes that have taken place in them.

 Remember, for this session, you'll need:

 To introduce the session:
Pictures of Queen Elizabeth's coronation.

 Activity and special place:
A selection of oils and creams: suntan lotion antiseptic cream, bath oil, vegetable oil, and so on.
For your special place, you will need the orange/red cloth, the icon of Jesus, or perhaps one that depicts Pentecost and, instead of the icon of Jesus, a crucifix, a candle and tongues of fire with headbands.

 Music:
• Daniel Iverson's "Spirit of the living God, fall afresh on me".
• Peter Scholes "We are one in the Spirit". There are a number of versions of this on YouTube; and, if you have a projector, you can show one of the videos.

 Other:
Widgit download ICYF 2 has Pentecost lotto and before/after Pentecost sorting activity which could support the themes and message of this session (http://www.widgit.com/resources/curriculum/re/i_call_you_friends/index.htm).

Meeting Christ
in the sacrament of reconciliation

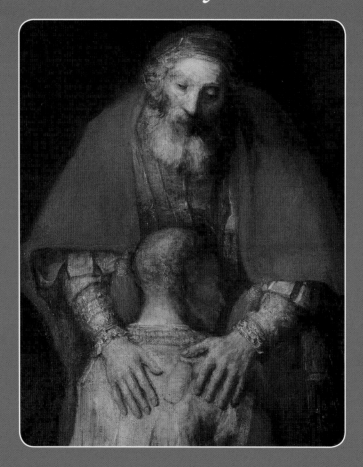

Preparing to celebrate the sacrament

9. Making loving choices

 Session aim To introduce God's "laws", the commandments, and how they help us make loving choices.

Preparing for the session

In this session, we are reminded that Jesus loves us very much. In fact, he wants us to know that he loves us so much there is nothing we can do to separate us from his love (Romans 8:39). This concept is difficult for most of us to grasp, no matter how young or how old we are, although, young children and people with learning disabilities can sometimes have less difficulty in accepting the concept of unconditional love. This session and the next couple of sessions can be used to prepare people for the sacrament of reconciliation and you should keep that concept in the front of your mind and in your heart as you prepare for this session. We will talk about the rules God has given us to help us be loving people. Think about how rules are made to protect us.

Exodus 19:1-6

1 *On the third new moon after the Israelites had gone out of the land of Egypt,*
   on that very day, they came into the wilderness of Sinai.
2 *They had journeyed from Rephidim, entered the wilderness of Sinai,*
   and camped in the wilderness;
   Israel camped in the wilderness there in front of the mountain.
3 *Then Moses went up to God; the Lord called to him from the mountain,*
   saying: "Thus you shall say to the house of Jacob, and tell the Israelites:
   You have seen what I did to the Egyptians,
   and how I bore you on eagles wings and brought you to myself.
5 *Now, therefore, if you obey my voice and keep my covenant,*
   you shall be my treasured possession out of all the peoples.
   Indeed, the whole earth is mine,
6 *but you shall be for me a priestly kingdom and a holy nation.*
   These are the words that you shall speak to the Israelites."

I chose this passage from Exodus 19 because I think it is important to understand that (in it and in Exodus 20), God was setting the Ten Commandments in the framework of

Facing page:
Harmenszoon van Rijn Rembrandt, detail from the *Return of the Prodigal Son*, (c. 1669), The Hermitage, St Petersburg

Reflect:

In Session 1, you were invited to reflect on the fact that, in Isaiah 43, God calls us precious. In this reading, God tells us that we are his treasured possessions. What does that mean to you and for you?

grace. If you don't understand that, you cannot understand the doctrinal importance of this passage. Israel did not earn this relationship with God, they did not deserve this relationship; it was a free gift.

The reading refers to the Jews as the chosen people. It describes them as a holy nation, God's own priests because of the covenant God made with them. St Peter reminded the early Christians about this in his first letter (1 Peter 2:9), and it is worth our while to be reminded that we, too, are God's treasured possessions.

The Catechism

When Jesus was asked, "Which commandment of the Law is the greatest?" he replied: "You shall love the Lord your God with all your heart, and with all your soul and with all your mind. This is the greatest and first commandment. And a second is like it: You shall love your neighbour as yourself. On these two commandments hangs all the Law." The Ten Commandments must be interpreted in light of this twofold yet single commandment of love (CCC 2055). You might say that loving God is loving your neighbour and loving your neighbour is loving God.

By way of preparing yourself for this session, take some quiet time reflecting on an experience in your life where you have loved someone gratuitously. You might find this prayer based on Psalm 139 helpful:

> "I stand before you, Lord, not knowing how to talk to you,
> and so I rely on the words with which you have inspired your prophets:
> Yahweh, you examine me and know me, you understand my thoughts from afar.
> You know every detail about me. Be with me and love me just as I am
> and help me to do the same with those I meet today."

God gave us the ten commandments (Exodus 20:1-17); and they are laws of respect and love. God helps us to know right choices from wrong ones by placing a small voice inside us to help us called a conscience.

Leading the session

Welcome

As always, the session begins with the welcome of each person by name, saying something like: "Welcome [name]. It is good to see you today!" In this session, we will be talking about the kind of rules people who love us make so that we can be safe and happy. You might ask which rules people are happy to follow, and which ones they don't like to follow. You might write on a paper "prize ribbon" the rules they follow best and present the ribbons later in the session.

The human dimension
(the activity drawing on our life experience)

We will be looking at rules that help us be more loving people. One of the most famous sets of rules is the ten commandments. We will be learning about them by making a copy of the tablets God gave to Moses. They and the prize ribbons will be the symbols we take to our special place.

There are various ways you can do this activity. You might get the participants to cut out the tablets from the activity book on the CD, or you might print out each of the commandments on a slip of paper (or card) with Velcro on the back. Have a strip of Velcro on the tablets and get people to place commandments onto the stones.

While you are doing this, you can talk about the different commandments and invite conversation from the participants about what they think these laws mean. Give people examples. Imagine the scene: a boy with a toy nearby. The girl was not interested in the toy he is playing with until he began to play with it. Then she wanted it just because he had it.

1. Love God with all your heart
2. Do not swear
3. Go to church on Sunday with your parish community
4. Love and obey your parents and carers
5. Respect others; do not fight with them.

6. Respect your body and other's bodies
7. Do not steal
8. Do not tell lies
9. Be thankful for your friends and family
10. Be thankful for what you have and share with others

There are two things we can use as a talking point here:

1. We've all experienced this feeling of envying what someone else has.
2. We are all faced with being asked to share something we have. Sometimes that is easy; sometimes it is not.

The big challenge for all of us is to be able to see ourselves honestly; to see when we are being loving, to know that Jesus is speaking to us and inviting to do the loving thing.

The religious dimension
(in the special place where Jesus speaks to us)

Lighting the candle

We light the candle to remind us that Jesus is the light in our lives and he is here with us. He shines the light so that we can see when we have been loving and when we have not.

Greeting the scripture

I am suggesting that, to greet the scripture, you use "Open my eyes, Lord" by James Manibusan, in this session and for the next two sessions:

> Open my eyes Lord, help me to see your face.
> Open my eyes Lord, help me to see.
> Open my ears Lord, help me to hear your voice.
> Open my ears Lord, help me to hear
> Open my heart Lord, help me to love like you.
> Open my heart Lord, help me to love

Sign our heads, mouths and hearts

Remind people we do this because we hear God's word in our heads, proclaim it with our mouths and feel it in our hearts.

Listening to Jesus in the scripture

Holding the book, speak reverently and clearly and read the scripture to the whole group. We suggest using this simplified version of Exodus 19:1-6.

When the people of Israel were camping in the desert,
Moses went up the mountain to talk to God.
God told Moses to tell his people:
"They saw for themselves what I did for them.
I saved them from the Egyptians and brought them here safely.
Just like an eagle carries her young ones on her wings.
If they will listen to my voice and keep my covenant,
they will be more precious to me than anyone else.
They will be my own priests, and they will have a holy nation."

Note:

For people who have difficulty in listening to a long Gospel, use only the last four lines of this scripture replacing the line that begins "If they will" with "God told Moses, 'if people will listen to my voice and do as I say…'"

Giving the scripture message to each person

Now approach each member of the group individually, saying:

> "[Name] Jesus says to you today:
> Do as I say and make loving choices."

Reading the scripture again to the whole group

After each person has heard Jesus speaking to them, the message is then given to the whole group.

Breaking the scripture open

People will probably know about rules they have to follow for games, such as card games, playground games, tag, hide-and-seek, outdoor and indoor types, hopscotch, jump rope and skipping rope rhymes. Ask if they know why these rules are there. Do they make the games safe and fun for them? Remember at the beginning of the session when they were asked which rules they follow best. They may voice their thoughts or they may think in the silence of their hearts. Remind them that God says we are precious to him. Ask them what it is like to be precious to someone. Ask them why their parents and friends who are precious to them want them to obey the rules that will keep them safe.

Close this part of the session

Bring this part of the session to a close with some music.
The words of Carey Landry's "I will never forget you, my people" work well:

I will never forget you my people, I have carved you on the palm of My hand,
I will never forget you, I will not leave you orphaned, I will never forget my own…
Does a mother forget her baby, or a woman the child within her womb,
Yet even if these forget, yes even if these forget, I will never forget my own.

This is a catchy tune and it would be a good one to get people involved in with percussion instruments if possible. When everyone is finished, you are now ready to move to the place where you will celebrate. You might make holy cards with an image to show we are carved on the palm of God's hand (which you can easily find on the internet) as a memento of this session.

Getting the message

Give people time to hear Jesus is saying that to them today, and perhaps you might ask them what they want to say to him.

Sharing the message/celebrating

It's time to celebrate; to share the Good News with one another. It is time for people to share with one another what this time together has been like for them, what they were feeling about God telling them that they are precious. You might also ask them if they feel differently about rules now that they know that the aim of the rule is to keep them safe.

✓ **Remember, for this session, you will need:**

✓ **To introduce the session:**
Ideas you can share about following rules or finding them hard to follow.

✓ **Activity and special place:**
Tablets for the ten commandments: You will have to choose how you want to make them; that is, card and paper; laminated card if you have the facility to do that, Velcro or scissors and glue, or prepared cards with the commandments on if the participants cannot use scissors.
For your special place, you will need a purple cloth, the icon of Jesus, candle, holy book.

✓ **Music:**
• Percussion instruments if you have them.
• James Manibusan's, "Open my eyes, Lord".
• Carey Landry's, "I will never forget you, my people".

10. What would Jesus do?

Session aim To introduce the concept of thinking about what Jesus would do, and choosing to do that.

Preparing for the session

Remember that we said in the last session that St Paul wrote to the Romans telling them that "God loves us so much there is nothing we can do to separate us from his love" (Romans 8:39). We continue to be inspired by this promise of God's unconditional love. All of us, no matter what age we are and what abilities or disabilities we have need God's unconditional love.

Love is an abstract concept. As with many things in relation to faith formation, you need to find concrete examples to share with people. One example that comes to mind: think about a time when someone joined a group you belong to, perhaps, they came to work in your office. Did you not want to include that new person because you didn't like the look of them or because they reminded you of someone you didn't like? Or, perhaps, you were the "new person". If you were the person who was not accepted, what was it like? Now, think about what Jesus would have done in the same circumstances.

Read:

Romans 8:31-39 and spend some time thinking about what St Paul said in his letter to the Romans: "God loves us so much there is nothing we can do to separate us from his love."

A boy excluded from the group in the near distance

Photo: Diana Klein

Luke 19:1-10

1 *Jesus entered Jericho and was passing through it.*
2 *A man there was named Zacchaeus: he was a chief tax collector and was rich.*
3 *He was trying to see who Jesus was,*
   but on account of the crowd he could not because he was short in stature.
4 *So he ran ahead and climbed a sycamore tree to see him, because he was going to pass that way.*
5 *When Jesus came to the place, he looked up and said to him:*
   "Zacchaeus, hurry and come down, for I must stay at your house today."
6 *So he hurried down and was happy to welcome him.*
7 *All who saw it began to grumble and said:*
   "He has gone to be the guest of one who is a sinner."
8 *Zacchaeus stood there and said to the Lord:*
   "Look, half of my possessions, Lord, I will give to the poor; and if I have defrauded anyone of anything, I will pay back four times as much."
9 *Then Jesus said to him: "Today salvation has come to this house,*
   because he too is a son of Abraham.
10 *For the Son of Man came to seek out and to save the lost.*

In this story, we don't see any evidence of faith on Zacchaeus' part; it sounds like he only wants to see Jesus out of curiosity. Maybe he climbed the sycamore tree not only because he was short, but because nobody wanted to stand next to him. It was Jesus who initiated his encounter with Zacchaeus, not the other way around.

In this story of Zacchaeus, the little man's life was changed as a result of his encounter with Jesus. Notice how Jesus offers communion with Zacchaeus before Zacchaeus' conversion. He does not make Zacchaeus' conversion a condition of the meal with him. The conversion took place as a result of Zacchaeus' contact with Jesus. This is a good example of how Jesus treated people and how he is inviting us to treat people. When we are faced with a choice about how to treat someone, we should ask ourselves the question: "What would Jesus do?"

The Catechism

Contemplate, as a children of God, on the forgiven sinner who agrees to welcome the love by which he is loved, and who wants to respond to it by loving even more (CCC 2712, Cf. Lk 7:36-50; 19:1-10).

By way of preparing yourself for this session, take some quiet time reflecting on an experience in your life where you responded to the love someone offered gratuitously to you by loving them even more in return. I suggest you use the prayer we used in the last session based on Psalm 139.

> I stand before you, Lord, not knowing how to talk to you,
> and so I rely on the words with which you have inspired your prophets:
> Yahweh, you examine me and know me, you understand
> my thoughts from afar. You know every detail about me.
> Be with me and love me just as I am and help me
> to do the same with those I meet today.

Leading the session

Welcome

As always, the session begins with the welcome of each person by name, saying something like: "Welcome [name]. It is good to see you today!" In this session, we will be talking about the kind of choices Jesus made and how we can try to make those same choices. You might ask the group to think of a time when someone new joined their group. It may have been a class at school or a group in a club. There is something different about this person; and, nobody likes him/her. Ask them if they chose to invite the person to join them or if they chose to exclude the person. Ask how they felt about it? Then, ask them if they have ever been the one who is excluded, and if so, how did they feel about it?

The human dimension
(the activity drawing on our life experience)

In this session, we are going to explore how our conscience works by asking a series of questions. People are likely to know the answers to the questions:

- "When I get cross with someone, I kick my dog." [Pause] then ask: "What do you think about that? Is it OK to kick the dog? Would Jesus do that?"
- "If I have broken something and I am asked about it, I say: 'I don't know anything about that! I didn't do it!'" [Pause] then ask: "What do you think about that? Is it OK to lie? Would Jesus do that?"
- "When I see someone with a mobile phone that I like, I take it away from them." [Pause] then ask: "What do you think about that? Is it right to steal? Would Jesus do that?"

To make WWJD bracelets: Cut light card or heavy paper into ¾" (2cm) wide strips 8" (20cm) long. Write the initials WWJD onto the strip. Glue or clip the strip to make a bracelet.

Think of some other scenarios that will apply to the people in your group. That little voice inside us helps us to know right from wrong. You might say it is God dwelling within us and guiding us. Depending on the ability of your people, you might then act out a few scenarios, asking the question at the end of each: "What would Jesus do?" You will see that the scenarios are using the ten commandments, which people learned about in the previous session.

1. Get people to act out a scene where two or three people are talking to each other and one person is left out. Pause for a moment and then ask: "What would Jesus do? Would he exclude that person?"
2. Give two people each a mobile phone. One of the phones could be old-fashioned and simple and the other could be the latest model. Get each of them to pretend to be happy with their gift, that is, until the one with the old-fashioned phone sees the modern one and she throws her phone on the floor saying she doesn't want it any more. Pause for a moment and then ask again: "What would Jesus do? Would he be jealous of the better phone?"
3. Two people are watching television and one person has control over the remote control and will not let the other choose any programme s/he wants to watch. Pause for a moment and then ask again: "What would Jesus do? Would he only think of himself or would he consider what the other person wants to watch?"
4. Give each participant a "What would Jesus do?" ("WWJD") bracelet, or make one. It will help people think of the question before they decide what to do.

The religious dimension
(in the special place where Jesus speaks to us)

Moving to the special place

The symbols you will carry to the special place are the bracelets with WWJD on them. If people are wearing their bracelets, you can either bring an extra one or make a sign with WWJD on it.

Lighting the candle

We light the candle to remind us that Jesus is the light in our lives and he is here with us helping us to see in our darkness.

Greeting the scripture

I suggest that you use James Manibusan's, "Open my eyes, Lord" again to greet the scripture. Using it in the two sessions about the sacrament and during the celebration of the sacrament to help to learn it:

> Open my eyes Lord, help me to see your face.
> Open my eyes Lord, help me to see.
> Open my ears Lord, help me to hear your voice.
> Open my ears Lord, help me to hear.
> Open my heart Lord, help me to love like you.
> Open my heart Lord, help me to love.

Sign your head, mouth and heart

Remind people we do this because we think about God's word, we proclaim it with our mouths and feel it in our hearts.

Read the scripture

Holding the book, speak reverently and clearly and read the scripture to the whole group. We suggest using this simplified version of the Gospel of Luke 19:1-10

> There was a man called Zacchaeus who really wanted to see Jesus.
> Many other people also came out to see Jesus and Zacchaeus
> was too short to see — so he climbed a sycamore tree and waited for Jesus to pass.
> When Jesus came to the place, he looked up and said: "Zacchaeus,
> I want to come to your house for lunch."
> So he hurried down and was happy to welcome him.
> The other people were angry and said:
> "Look, Jesus, has chosen to stay in a sinner's house."
> But Zacchaeus said to Jesus: "Look, I will give half of what I own to the poor;
> and if I have cheated anyone out of money, I will pay back four times as much."
> Then Jesus said to him: "Today you have been saved.
> You, too, are of the family of Abraham. And I have come to find
> and save people like you who are lost."

Giving the scripture message to each person, saying,

"[Name] Jesus says to you today, I want to come to your house".

Alternative activity:

If you need an alternative to this (or if you need something different to break the scripture open), you will find a drawing of Zacchaeus with Jesus that you can invite people to colour in on the additional resources CD.

Note:

For people who have difficulty in listening to a long gospel, simplify and shorten this or adapt it as you think you need to. This is the kind of story they might be able to listen to though; it's not as complex as much of the scripture we hear.

Reading the scripture again to the whole group

After each person has heard Jesus speaking to them, the message is then given to the whole group.

Breaking the scripture open

I suggest that you use Henry Martin's cartoon version of the story of Zacchaeus on Sermons4Kids. Alternatively, this is always a good gospel for people to act if abilities allow. If you do, you will need a small step ladder and a large branch, a table and two chairs, some bread and juice (in a goblet if possible). If you want or need a script, make it up or find one on the internet. To help break open the scriptures on this occasion, you might begin by repeating the scripture message and ask: "What is your answer?"

Getting the message

Give people time to hear Jesus saying that he wants to go to their house. Ask them what they will say to Jesus and give them time to think.

Sharing the message

It's time to celebrate. Remember how important this part of the session is. It's a time to share the Good News with one another, to affirm one another. You might use the bread and juice from Jesus' and Zacchaeus' meal and get people to imagine that they have joined Zacchaeus and Jesus at their meal. Ask them what they would say to Zacchaeus and what they might say to Jesus. One way of doing this would be let them take turns pretending to be Zacchaeus and Jesus, as if they are in a "hot seat" and get people to engage in conversation with them.

✓ **Remember, for this session, you'll need:**

✓ **To introduce the session:**
Stories of people being excluded and asking what Jesus would do.

✓ **Activity and special place:**
• "What would Jesus do?" bracelets, or the materials you will need to make them (paper, glue, marker pens to write WWJD on them).
• The PowerPoint presentation from Sermons 4Kids (www.sermons4kids.com) if you have the facilities to use it. It allows free use for ministry purposes. If you decide to act it out, you will need a step ladder, a large branch, a table, two chairs, some bread, goblets and some juice.
• For your special place, you will need the usual cloths , icon, candle, holy book.

✓ **Music:**
• James Manibusan's "Open my eyes, Lord". There are several versions on YouTube. My favourite is by CJM Music, but you'll need to buy the CD to hear it.

Celebration:
The second step on the journey

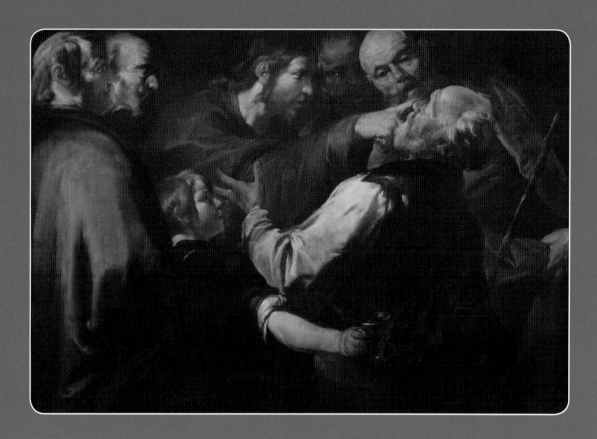

Jesus helps us see what's in our hearts
in the rites of blessing and healing

Celebration: Jesus helps us see what's in our hearts – the scrutiny or penitential rite

For the baptised to have a good experience of celebrating the sacrament of reconciliation; for those preparing for baptism, to celebrate the scrutiny.

Preparing for the session

In this session, the baptised people will celebrate the sacrament of reconciliation; the unbaptised people will celebrate the scrutiny (a word that refers to the self-searching) of those asking for baptism. This is the second step towards the sacraments of initiation for them. The scrutiny is designed to heal all that is weak and sinful in the hearts of the candidates and to strengthen all that is upright and good.

The ability of those who are baptised to search themselves is also important as they ask to celebrate the sacrament of reconciliation.

By way of preparing yourself for this session, spend some time reflecting on what your reaction is to what Pope Francis said and think about your own experience of celebrating the sacrament of reconciliation. He reminded us in a homily he gave recently us that, "in this sacrament, we meet Jesus and feel his tenderness". Is this your experience?

John 9:1-12

1   *As Jesus walked along, he saw a man blind from birth.*
2   *His disciples asked him: "Rabbi, who sinned, this man or his parents that he was born blind?"*
3   *Jesus answered: "Neither this man nor his parents sinned, he was born blind so that God's works might be revealed in him.*
4   *We must work the works of him who sent me while it is day; Night is coming when no one can work.*
5   *As long as I am in the world, I am the light of the world."*
6   *When he said this, he spat on the ground and made mud with the saliva and spread the mud on the man's eyes,*

Overleaf:
Gioacchino Assereto
Christ healing the blind man, c. 1640
(Carnegie Museum)

116

7 *Saying to him: "Go and wash In the pool of Siloam (which means sent). Then he went and washed and came back able to see.*

8 *The neighbours and those who had seen him before as a beggar began to ask: "Is this not the man who used to sit and beg?"*

9 *Some were saying: "It is he." Others were saying: "No, but it is someone like him." But he kept saying: "I am the man."*

10 *But they kept asking him: "Then how were your eyes opened?"*

11 *He answered: "The man called Jesus made mud, spread it on my eyes, and said to me: "Go to Siloam and wash. Then I went and washed and received my sight."*

12 *They said to him: "Where is he?" He said: "I do not know."*

This man used to sit and beg all day. It was the only way he could get any money since he could not work. The Jews thought that he or his parents must have sinned; and that was why he was blind. Jesus told them that they were wrong. He was born blind so that Jesus could heal him. The blind man didn't know who Jesus was or what really happened. He only knew that he was blind and then he could see.

But, the important point in the story was not only that after Jesus had cured him, he could see with his eyes; but that he had insight. He could see with his heart and he could see that Jesus came from God. He said a sinner could not do such a miraculous thing. The pharisees, however, couldn't see. Like the pharisees, we can be very blind to our faults and weaknesses; and, like the pharisees, even when people point them out, we sometimes still refuse to see.

The Catechism tells us

Often Jesus asks the sick to believe. He makes use of signs to heal: spittle and the laying on of hands, mud and washing. The sick try to touch him, "for power came forth from him and healed them all". In the sacraments, Christ continues to "touch" us in order to heal us. (CCC1504). We say in the Lord's Prayer, " Thy will be done". If we are worshipers of God, we should want to do his will (CCC2827).

The priest acts in *persona Christi*

It is important for us to believe and accept that, in the sacrament of reconciliation, the priest makes Christ present. Pope John Paul II called the priest a merciful bridge-builder, faithful and compassionate pastor dedicated to search for the lost sheep, the doctor who heals and comforts, the one teacher who teaches the truth and teaches the way of God (Pope John Paul II, *Apostolic Exhortation Reconiliatio et Paenitentia*, 1984, n. 29).

Note:

Leaders should be sensitive to the people they are working with. for example, if you are working with someone with an intellectual disability who is also blind. The emphasis is on the opening of the eyes of the heart. Beware of the perceived link between disability and sin. This scripture is the very one where Jesus denounces any such link.

By way of preparing yourself for this liturgy ask yourself how easy it is for you to accept and believe in the healing touch of Christ in the sacraments and consider celebrating the sacrament of reconciliation before this celebration.

Leading the liturgy

We have planned this liturgy using a similar format to the sessions since people will be familiar with it and will, therefore, be more comfortable.

Welcome

Begin this liturgy as you begin every session with the welcome in the meeting place. One difference: parents, godparents, catechists, priests and faith friends should be invited. The priest welcomes everyone and explains (in his own words) that today, everyone will hear the comforting message of God's love and forgiveness; but the people who are not yet baptised will celebrate the scrutiny, and those who are already baptised will celebrate the sacrament of reconciliation. (See RCIA271.)

The human dimension
(the activity drawing on our life experience)

In preparation to celebrate these rites, we suggest that each person in the group be given a leaf. If it is autumn, pick different coloured leaves that are supple enough for people to handle; otherwise, make leaves out of coloured paper. Put a branch into a pot with soil in it to hold it upright making it a tree for the leaves.

Moving to the special place

Carry the leaves to your special place and place them carefully on the focal point. Carry the branch and place it beside the focal point. Depending on the people in your group, you may use the church as your special place; but if people will be comfortable, you can use the special place they are used to. Either way, have a purple cloth on the focal point making a link between it and the stole that the priest is wearing.

Celebrating the rites
(in the special place where Jesus speaks to us)

Note:

Consider the idea of preparing a booklet for this liturgy using symbol supported text to assist with engagement and participation if possible. A booklet to help people who are able to read celebrate the sacrament of reconciliation in the future is included in the additional resources CD on pages 20–21.

Lighting the candle

Jesus is the light in our lives and he is here with us. He sheds light on us so that we can see.

Greeting the scripture

Pause here to sing James Manibusan's "Open my eyes, Lord" which will be familiar. if you've used it in the last couple of sessions. It is a way to greet the scripture and to get people to open themselves up to the Lord.

> Open my eyes Lord, help me to see your face
> Open my eyes Lord, help me to see.
> Open my ears Lord, help me to hear your voice.
> Open my ears Lord, help me to hear
> Open my heart Lord, help me to love like you
> Open my heart Lord, help me to love.

Sign our heads, mouths and hearts

Remind people we do this because we hear God's word in our heads, proclaim it with our mouths and feel it in our hearts.

Listening to Jesus in the scripture

> There was a blind man who used to sit begging all day;
> It was the only way he could get any money.
> The Jews thought he or his parents must have
> done something bad and that was why he was blind.
> Jesus told them that this was not true.
> Neither of them had done anything bad.
> He healed the blind man and suddenly he could see;
> but it was not just with is eyes he could see.
> Even though others could not see, the blind man
> could see that it was Jesus who healed him.
> He knew that only a very good man could do that.

Simplify this Gospel if you need to, perhaps like this: There was a blind man whose only way of getting money was to beg. Jesus saw him and felt sorry for him so he cured him and let him see with his eyes; but this man could also see with his heart. He knew Jesus was a very good man.

The priest gives a short homily

He might talk about how we are often blind to our faults until someone points them out to us. Even then, it is sometimes hard to see that we are doing something that is not loving. We might be fighting with someone. We believe we are right and we will not see their point of view. It isn't easy sometimes to admit that we might be wrong. Sometimes it's not easy to say "sorry" even when we know we are wrong.

Giving the scripture message to each person

"[Name] Jesus tells you today, I will help you to see what you need to change so that you can become more like me."

Now, the priest says to the whole group:

"Jesus wants to heal us of our blindness,
to help us to see when we have not been loving as he is."

After a very brief silence, the priest will say:

Note:

I have incorporated part of the rite of election here. It is not included in the adapted rite for older children (which is what we have based these rites on) but I think it is good to include it for people with learning disabilities since some of them will be adults. If it is possible for them to attend the rite of election at the cathedral, though, that would be infinitely preferable. If that is possible, you should ignore the section included here.

"Dear parents, godparents, catechists and friends:
The people here present have asked to participate more fully
in the sacramental life of the Church. Can you tell me:
Have they shown a sincere desire to follow Jesus?
R/: They have.
Have they listened well to the word of God?
R/: They have.
Are they trying to live as followers of Jesus?
R/: They are.
Are they taking part in the community's life of service and prayer?
R/: They are.

(adapted from RCIA 118-119)

Dear friends, will you offer them the support of your love and concern,
and above all, be good models to them of Christian living so that
by your example, they may grow deeper in the faith of the Church?
R/: we will. All respond: Amen

We will now celebrate the scrutiny and sacrament of reconciliation.

Even though they will try to live as your children,
they will sometimes find this difficult.

120

They want to walk with you, Jesus.
If they stumble on the way, and do not please you,
help them up with the power of your hand
that they may continue on their journey to you
with Jesus Christ, our Lord."

(adapted from RCIA 276)

Anointing with the oil of catechumens (or the laying on of hands)

The rite continues with the unbaptised people being anointed with oil. The priest says:

"I anoint you with the oil of salvation in the name of Jesus.
May he strengthen you with his power who lives for ever and ever."

Or, for the Laying on of hands, he says:

"May Jesus strengthen you with his power
For he is Lord for ever and ever."

(adapted from RCIA 277)

An examination of conscience

[Pause for a moment of silence.] The leader then says, "Let's think about the times when we have stumbled":

- Maybe there was a time when we were sad because we upset someone. We might also be sad because we didn't want to say "sorry".
- Maybe there was a time when we refused to share something with others; we wanted it all to ourselves.
- Maybe there was a time when we lied about something we did, so we would not get into trouble and someone else got in trouble instead.
- Showing the tree (the branch in the pot) with no leaves, the priest or leader says: "It looks like there is no life on this tree. Sometimes, we feel like this tree. It looks sad. Sometimes we are sad and do not have much life in us."

[Pause for some silence.]

During the Anointing or the laying on of hands:

You may play "Lay your hands" by Carey Landry. If it is too long for the attention span of your people, just play the first few lines:
"Lay your hands gently upon us. Let their touch render your peace.
Let them bring your forgiveness and healing, lay your hands, gently lay your hands."
If you have someone who can play it on a guitar, they can repeat these few lines over and over.

Liturgy of penance

Next the liturgy of the sacrament of penance begins for the baptised people who will celebrate this sacrament for the first time.

(adapted from RCIA 277)

The priest invites those who are already baptised and those who will be celebrating the sacrament to approach him and to tell him or show him in some way something they are sorry about. He will tell them that when they speak to him, they are speaking to Jesus. Jesus is there with us. He will then tell them that God forgives and he reminds them that God loves them very much.

Alternative act of contrition:

You will find a symbol supported text 'sorry prayer' available in ICYF/ Come and See Prayer pack, which can be downloaded from the Widgit website for a small fee (http://www.widgit.com/resources/curriculum/re/i_call_you_friends/index.htm).

You may need symbol support so that participants can lift and place in a basket next to a "Sorry Jesus" symbol—or so that they can point to symbols if this is the way they can communicate.

You will also find a leaflet on the additional resources CD to guide those who can read and follow it through the rite of penance.

Act of contrition

The leader continues, encouraging everyone to repeat where they can:

> "O my God, I am very sorry
> that I am not always as loving
> as you want me to be;
> but, with your help,
> I know I can put things right
> and I can be more loving. Amen"

Penance

To show we really want to be move loving, Jesus gave us a prayer to say:

> Our Father, who art in heaven, hallowed be thy name.
> Thy kingdom come, thy will be done on earth as it is in heaven.
> Give us this day our daily bread and forgive us our trespasses
> as we forgive those who trespass against us
> and lead us not into temptation but deliver us from evil. Amen.

The priest or the leader draws attention to the tree that seems to have no life in it. He gives a leaf to each person, inviting them to put them on the branches. The tree now seems to come alive. When we reconnect ourselves to Jesus in the sacrament, we too feel a sense of new life. We remember that there is nothing that can separate us from him.

Photo: Diana Klein

Sign of peace

The priest says: "We are now happy. Let's reach out to grasp the hand of God and to shake each others' hands, as we say: "Peace be with you!" While offering the sign of peace, sing: "Shalom, my friend, Shalom my friend, Shalom, shalom, the peace of Christ I give you today." This will also double as the closing hymn for the liturgy.

Celebrating and sharing the message

Remember how important it is for people to have this time together as their friendships grow. They have shown their vulnerable side to each other and it is especially important for them to know they are still loved by their new friends even though they've admitted they have faults. This is a special celebration both for the baptised and unbaptised. It is special, too, because parents, godparents and faith friends are present. Ask people to bring and share some food and drink that are, perhaps, a little more special than usual.

 Remember, for this session, you'll need:
You may want to make a liturgy booklet for the participants and their parents, godparents and carers.

 To introduce the session:
Leaves (dried or paper).

 Activity and special place:
You will need the purple cloth, icon, candle, holy book, a dry branch, the leaves (dried or paper), flowers and a pot and something to attach the leaves and flowers to the branch.

 Music:
• James Manibusan's "Open my eyes, Lord".
• "Shalom, my friend, shalom". Hear it on YouTube.
• "Lay your hands" by Carey Landry. Hear it on YouTube.

Meeting Christ in the Mass

Preparing to celebrate the Eucharist

11. The Mass: Introductory rites
We gather and prepare

Session aim ▸ To understand that, even though we don't see him, Jesus is really present when we gather for Mass.

Preparing for the session

The aim of this session is to help people be aware that Jesus is really present when we gather in his name for Mass. This concept shouldn't be too hard for people to take on board since you've been encouraging them to be aware of Christ's presence during our prayer time in the first five sessions. The scripture we've chosen for this session is Jesus' promise to be with us when we gather in his name (Matthew 18:20). In this session, we will also reflect on how we prepare to meet him in the Mass — just as we prepare to meet people at the special meals we have at home when special friends come or when we are celebrating birthdays, weddings, and so on. The image of people gathered at a table tells the story of friendship. Tables are about presence and the quality of presence, our presence to one another and God's presence with us.

Matthew 18:15-20

15 *"If another member of the church sins against you, go and point out the fault when the two of you are alone. If the member listens to you, you have regained that one*

16 *But if you are not listened to, take one or two others along with you, so that every word may be confirmed by the evidence of two or three witnesses.*

17 *If the member refuses to listen to them, tell it to the church;*
and if the offender refuses to listen even to the church,
let such a one be to you as a Gentile and a tax collector.

18 *Truly I tell you, whatever you bind on earth will be bound in heaven,*
and whatever you loose on earth will be loosed in heaven.

19 *Again, truly I tell you, if two of you agree on earth about anything you ask,*
it will be done for you by my Father in heaven.

20 *For where two or three are gathered in my name, I am there among them."*

In this reading, we focus on our obligation to help one another grow in goodness.

Facing page:
The Mafu people are a North Cameroon ethnic group: this is their depiction of the Last Supper.

Sometimes, this means we have to point something out to our brother or sister at home, at school or in the church that they have to be corrected about. Jesus tells us that the leaders are not the only ones responsible for doing this; it applies to all of us. By saying that "where two or three are gathered in my name, I am there among them", Jesus is telling the community that it has power and authority. The source of that power is Jesus: "I am there among them."

We have all experienced being corrected by our parents and teachers when we were children, and by our managers or other authorities when we are adults, and it is not always a positive experience. Think about it. Jesus is teaching us that we need to talk over our differences while showing respect for the other, and he promises that he will be there with us to help us.

The Catechism

The Catechism tells us that it is the duty of Christians to take part in the life of the Church and impels them to act as witnesses of the Gospel and of the obligations that flow from it. It says that this witness is a transmission of the faith in words and deeds. Witness is an act of justice that establishes the truth or makes it known (CCC 2472; cf Matthew 18:16). Referring to the last verse of the Gospel: "Where two or three are gathered in my name, I am there among them", the Catechism tells us that Christ is always present in his Church, especially in her liturgical celebrations. He is present in four ways: through the ministry of the priest, in the eucharistic species, in the word and in the assembly when the Church prays and sings (CCC 1088).

By way of preparing yourself for this session take some time to continue reflecting on what it means to be Christ's witnesses. Think about the times when you have helped someone grow in goodness by your intervention. Think about the times when someone else has helped you to grow in goodness and consider sharing your reflection with the group or with one of the parents, priests or catechists.

Leading the session

Welcome

Every session begins with the welcome of each person by name. You might introduce the session by asking the participants what it is like to talk on the telephone. They know the person is at the other end of the phone; they can talk with one another and listen to one another, even though they cannot see one another. When we pray, when we come to Mass, we know Jesus is there too, even though we cannot see him.

The human dimension
(the activity drawing on our life experience)

In this session, we suggest that you ask the participants to think about what they do to prepare for a special meal. It might be special because good friends are coming or you might be celebrating a birthday or a wedding. Ask them what they put on the table and then get them to set a table with a white table cloth, candles, flowers, nice dishes and wine glasses. If possible, have bread and wine or grape juice for the table too. (You might include some multi-sensory items to help.)

Moving to the special place

Have an altar cloth, a chalice, a ciborium, a jug of altar wine or juice, some hosts, a candle and some flowers in the room where you meet. Make a ritual of getting people to carry these special things into the church or the special place where you are meeting.

The religious dimension
(in the special place where Jesus speaks to us)

Lighting the candle

We light the candle or candles on the altar to remind us that Jesus is the light of the world and he is here with us in the church (or in this special place) even though we cannot see him. Ask if they recall seeing those candles lit when they come to Mass.

Photo: Diana Klein

Greet the reading from scripture

I suggest the first two verses of Carey Landry's "Thank you Lord".

> Thank you Lord for giving us life; thank you Lord for giving us life —
> right where we are. Alleluia, praise the Lord! Right where we are.
> Thank you Lord for giving us love; thank you Lord for giving us love —
> right where we are. Alleluia, praise the Lord! Right where we are.

Read the scripture

Holding the book, speak reverently and clearly and read the scripture to the whole group. We suggest using this adapted version of the Gospel of Matthew 18:15-20

If your brother or sister does something wrong, go and talk to him or her on your own.
If they listen to you and stop what they were doing, you have helped them.
But if they don't listen to you, take two or three other people with you and try again.
If the person will not listen to them either, go tell it to the Christian community.
And if they won't even listen to them either,
then that person just wants to go on doing the wrong thing.
Then Jesus said: "I tell you honestly,
whenever two or three of you agree to pray about something,
God will listen. For wherever two or three people
are gathered in my name, I am there with them."

Giving the scripture message to each person

Now approach each member of the group individually, holding their hands and looking into their eyes, saying, "[name] Jesus tells you today:

When you are with two or three others in my name, I am really there with you."

Reading the scripture again to the whole group

After each person has heard Jesus speaking to them, the message is then given to the whole group again. Remember how important it is to do this with a wide gesture, which includes everyone. It helps each person to feel they are part of the group as well as being an equal member of a community in which God is present.

Breaking the scripture open

Earlier in this session, we talked about how we prepare when we are celebrating a special meal. The church needs to be prepared when we go to Mass too because it is also a special meal. Get people to "set" the altar table with the cloth, chalice, a ciborium, a jug of altar wine (if possible) or juice, some hosts and some flowers. They can use the altar candle. (They should be familiar with these special items from session 4.)

We do other things to prepare to meet Jesus at Mass, for example:

- As Mass begins on Sundays, we do certain things altogether. We sing a hymn together; then we all make the sign of the cross together. This helps us feel that we are one people, the Body of Christ;
- We remember the times when we have not been as loving as we should be, when we have not forgiven someone. In the Gospel we just heard, Jesus teaches us about forgiveness. He says that if we have a disagreement with someone, we should try to make things right. It is like wanting to make up with one another if we've had a disagreement, before we celebrate a special meal;
- We sing the Gloria (most Sundays) to show that we are happy that, even when we have disagreements with others, even when we are fighting with others, God will always forgive us;
- God provides us with everything we need. Jesus invites us to remember that and to celebrate with him at his table. You might listen to or sing the chorus of "Come to the feast".

    "Come to the feast of heaven and earth! Come to the table of plenty!
    God will provide for all that we need, here at the table of plenty!"

Mgr Vincent Harvey, St Joseph and St Edmund's Parish, Southampton

Getting the message

Give people time to hear Jesus is saying that to them today. Remind them that Jesus is there with them wanting to say something to them. After a pause, ask them if they want to share what that is.

Close this part of the session

Bring this part of the session to a close with some quiet prayer. Something along these lines might work for your group: "Jesus, you promised that you would be with us when we gather together in your name and we trust you to keep your promise. Help us to feel you with us now and always. Amen." When everyone is finished, you are now ready to move to where you will celebrate.

Sharing the message/celebrating

You might begin today's celebration with the last two verses of Carey Landry's song thanking God for giving us joy and for giving us (choose something) right where we are. It's a catchy tune which says everything you want to say as you celebrate and share the Good News with one another. You might give people percussion instruments to join in with the music. By now in the programme, people will be ready to thank God for one another. Friendships have begun to develop and the time spent together has (hopefully) become a time of joy. If possible, sit at the table you set at the start of the session fill it with everything you used during the session.

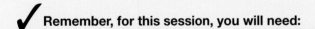

Remember, for this session, you will need:

To introduce the session:
You might have a mobile phone handy if you think you need it.

Activity:
A table that you can set with a white table cloth and napkins, candles and flowers, nice dishes and wine glasses, If possible, have bread and wine or grape juice, multi-sensory items that might be used for celebrations.In the church (or the special place), you will need: an altar cloth, a chalice, a ciborium, a jug of altar wine (if possible), some hosts, an altar candle (or two) and some flowers. And, as always, the holy book with the simplified reading placed inside.

Music:
Several versions of it are available on YouTube.
• Carey Landry's "Thank you God" for the acclamation and the celebration.
• "Come to the feast of heaven and earth" by Daniel Schutte.

12. The Mass: We listen
(The Liturgy of the Word)

 Session aim When we listen to people, we get to know them. We get to know Jesus when we listen to him speaking to us in the scriptures.

Preparing for the session

Think about what a rugby team looks like as it huddles before they begin to play. The players listen to one another and they listen to the coach. They help one another to decide what their next move is. This is how they decide how they will play the game and who will do what. Listening is very important when you are a part of a any family, team, community.

Luke 10:38-40

[38] *"Now as they went on their way,*
Jesus entered a certain village,
where a woman named Martha
welcomed him into her home.
[39] *She had a sister named Mary, who sat at the Lord's feet*
and listened to what he was saying.
[40] *But Martha was distracted by her many tasks;*
so she came to Jesus and asked:
'Lord, do you not care that
my sister has left me to do all the work by myself?
Tell her then to help me.'
[41] *But the Lord answered her: 'Martha, Martha,*
you are worried and distracted by many things;
[42] *there is need of only one thing.*
Mary has chosen the better part,
which will not be taken away from her.'"

In this reading, we focus on listening to God's Word. Martha is busy doing lots of things. Mary, on the other hand, sits at Jesus' feet to listen to what he has to say to her. Jesus is not making the point that doing things for others is not important. That would go against the

Note:

You might have some pictures of rugby teams huddled together before they begin to play.

Gospel message that we should listen to God's Word and we should act on it.

The point here is that we must listen to Jesus in our hearts so that we can hear what he is saying to us about the way he wants us to live. We have to listen and think about what he is saying if we want to be like him. We have to listen to him and notice the way he treated people, the way he helped people, the way he loved people because it is only by getting to know him well that we can be like him.

The Catechism

The Catechism tells us that Samuel would have learned from his mother, Hannah, how to "stand before the Lord" and that Samuel learned from Eli to listen to God's Word (CCC 2578). Likewise, it is our responsibility as parents, priests and catechists to take care in the way we teach others to "stand before the Lord" and to listen to his word.

The Catechism goes on to tell us that in order to nourish people well with the Word of God, the signs that accompany it should be emphasised: the book of the Word, its veneration (the procession, incense, candles), the place of its proclamation, and making sure its reading is audible and intelligible in addition to the way it is broken open (CCC 1154). Lastly, we must remember that Christ is present in his Word. It is he who speaks when the holy scriptures are read in the church (CCC 1088). As Catholics, we believe this is true.

Reflect

As you prepare for this session, can you remember what Gospel you heard at Mass last Sunday?

By way of preparing yourself for this session, take some time to think about how you listen to the scripture being proclaimed during Mass. Are you paying as much attention as you would be if you really believe it is Jesus speaking to you in person?

Leading the session

Welcome

Every session begins with the welcome of each person by name and telling them how good it is to see them. In this session, you might say: "Jesus welcomes you today [name]. He is here with us and he has something to say to us, so listen carefully!"

The human dimension
(the activity drawing on our life experience)

In this session, we are reflecting on the importance of listening, especially listening to Jesus. I suggest we use the story of Samuel. Some of the catechists or faith friends may act it out.

Reader:	A long time ago, there was a priest called Eli. He was very old and he was going blind. A young boy called Samuel went to live in the temple to help Eli. One night when it was very quiet, Samuel heard a voice calling him.
Voice:	"Samuel, Samuel!"
Samuel:	Getting up and running to Eli said: "Here I am. Did you call me?"
Eli:	"No, I didn't call you. Go back to bed."
Samuel:	(Went back to bed; but he heard the voice calling him again. And, again, he went back to Eli and said:) "Here I am. Did you call me?"
Eli:	"No, I didn't call you. Go back to bed."
Samuel:	(Went back to bed again; but, again, he heard the voice calling him. And, again, he went back to Eli and said:) "Here I am. Did you call me?"
Eli:	"No, I didn't call you. Go back to bed."
Samuel:	(Went back to bed very confused; and, again, he heard the voice calling him. He went back to Eli and said:) "You did call me. I heard you!"
Reader:	This time, Eli realised that it was God calling Samuel, so he told him:
Eli:	"If you hear the voice again, say: 'Speak, Lord, I am listening.'"
Reader:	Samuel laid down and listened in the silence. Once again, God called Samuel. Voice: "Samuel, Samuel!"
Samuel:	(Did as Eli told him to. He said:) "Speak, Lord, I am listening."
Reader:	God gave Samuel a message for Eli. God said: "I am going to do something that will make people's ears tingle. I am going to do everything I told Eli I would do". It was the first of many times God spoke to him. Each time it happened, he passed the messages on to anyone who would listen.

If you don't want to act out the story, consider making hand (or finger puppets) and performing a puppet show. (You can copy these or other images of Samuel and Eli from the internet and put them on pop sticks or use them as finger puppets.) Conversations about how important listening is may just happen after acting out or hearing this story.

Note:

If you are acting the story out, you will need a bed (a makeshift one out of chairs will work) and Samuel and Eli will probably want to dress in albs or kaftans.

Moving to the special place

Set the place in the church with some chairs around the lectern at the front of the church. If you've used finger puppets, bring them to your special place; if people have acted the story out, bring something from the props you have used.

If possible, take a thurible to the special place along with the holy book. Light the incense and put it in the thurible if this is practical and ask people to carry the holy book and the thurible to the special place in procession. Using the sense of smell will help build anticipation for listening to the scripture. If it is not practical to use the parish thurible, you might use a censer (a small bowl) and put in it some granulated incense for home use.

You can get small, concave charcoal briquettes. You light the corner of the briquette, then place it in the censer and extinguish the flame. After the glowing sparks traverse the entire briquette, it is ready to have incense placed on it. Alternatively, censers made for stick incense are also available; these are simply a long, thin plate of wood, metal, or ceramic, bent up and perforated at one end to hold the incense; they serve to catch the ash of the burning incense stick.

This might be a good time to sing or listen to the chorus of Daniel Schutte's: "Here I am, Lord":

> "Here I am, Lord. Is it I, Lord? I have heard You calling in the night.
> I will go Lord, if You lead me. I will hold Your people in my heart."

The religious dimension
(in the special place where Jesus speaks to us)

Lighting the candle

Once people have settled and are quiet, light the candle. Ask people to sit and see if they can feel Jesus present with us.

Greeting the scripture

Our acclamations to greet the scripture can be more adaptable than they are at Mass. For this session, the chorus of Damien Lundy's: "Oh the word of my Lord" works well:

> Oh, the word of my Lord, deep within my being,
> oh the word of my Lord, you have filled my mind.

Sign our heads, mouths and hearts

Invite the others to do so too, as it will instil the idea that God's word enters our thoughts, we tell others about it and we feel it in our hearts.

Listening to Jesus in the scripture

Holding the book, speak reverently and clearly and read the scripture to the whole group. We suggest using this adapted version of the Gospel of Luke 10:38-42.

One day, Jesus was on a trip.
He came to a village where his friends Mary and Martha lived.
They welcomed him into their home
and Mary sat down with Jesus.
He talked to her and she listened.
Martha went into the kitchen to make
a meal for them.
She was doing all the work.
She was getting cross with Mary and
she said to Jesus: "Lord, do you not see
that I am doing all the work and my
sister is just sitting here listening to
you?"
Jesus replied: "Martha, Martha, you
worry about so many things. I know
it is important to make a meal; but
the most important thing is to be with
me and to listen to what I have to say.
Mary has chosen to listen to me and I
will not stop her from doing that."

drawing by Kim Blundeel © 2014

Giving the scripture message to each person

Now approach each member of the group individually, holding their hands and looking into their eyes, saying,

> "[Name] Jesus tells you today: The most important thing is to be with me and to listen to what I have to say. "

Reading the scripture again to the whole group

After each person has heard Jesus speaking to them, the message is then given to the whole group again.

Breaking the scripture open

You might consider having an activity with pictures or symbols of things people like to listen to; people they like listening to and the different ways they can listen to God (including through the scriptures). This might be done individually or it could be a shared activity with a faith friend. You might get them to colour in the picture of Jesus with Martha and Mary on the previous page (which you will find on the additional resources CD). While they are doing that, to talk about how they think each of the people in the picture was feeling, what they were thinking.

Getting the message

Remember to give people time to hear Jesus is speaking to them today.

Sharing the message/celebrating

Begin the celebration by repeating the words of the music "we come to share our story". You can use this as a conversation starter asking people what it is like to share their story, to talk to people who are interested in them. This is one of the most important things you do in the celebration at the end of the session. This is when people get the chance to know one another better by listening to each other's stories. That is just the point we are making in this session about Jesus too. We only come to know Jesus by listening to him, by listening to his story.

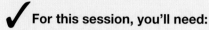 **For this session, you'll need:**

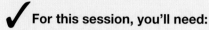 **To introduce the session:**
Images of a game where people listen to one another.

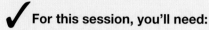 **Activity and special place:**
If you are going to act the story of Samuel and Eli out, you'll need props: maybe two beds and a screen (and the script), albs or night dresses for Samuel and Eli. If you are going to use finger puppets, you'll need to organise them. You will also need, as always: the holy book with the simplified reading placed inside, draped cloth, a candle. In the church, you will also need to arrange to use the lectern, the usual cloths and an Icon of Jesus, a candle that you can light, photos of people and religious images to help people choose who and what helps them listen and how listening helps them to hear other's stories.

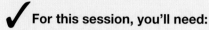 **Music:**
• Daniel Schutte's, "Here I am, Lord". The chords are on-line: http://music.kkihs.org/songs/details/here-i-am-lord.
• The tune of David Haas's chorus from "We come to share our story".
• Damien Lundy's, "Oh, the word of my Lord".

photo by Diana Klein

137

13. The Mass: we offer bread and wine (the liturgy of the Eucharist)

Session aim

To learn that we offer bread and wine and we offer ourselves. The bread and wine are changed and we are changed.

Preparing for the session

In this session, we will be talking about how we offer the bread and wine and how they are transformed into the Body and Blood of Jesus. In the same way, we offer ourselves and we, too, are transformed so that we can take Jesus out to the people we meet. We've chosen the Gospel of the miracle at Cana. We will aim to show that two individuals offer themselves to each other and, because of that, they change. They are no longer two separate people; they have been joined in marriage, they are a couple. They think of the other, often before themselves.

John 2:1-11

1 *"On the third day a wedding took place at Cana in Galilee and the mother of Jesus was there.*
2 *Jesus and his disciples had also been invited to the wedding.*

Photo © Diana Klein

138

³ *When the wine gave out, the mother of Jesus said to him: "They have no wine."*
⁴ *"Woman, what concern is that to you and me?*
My hour has not yet come."
⁵ *His mother said to the servants: "Do whatever he tells you."*
⁶ *Now standing there were six stone water jars for the Jewish rites*
of purifications, each holding from twenty to thirty gallons.
⁷ *Jesus said to them: "Fill the jars with water";*
and they filled them to the brim.
⁸ *He said to them: "Now draw some out and take it to the chief steward." So, they took it.*
⁹ *When the steward tasted the water that had become wine.*
He did not realise where it had come from,
though the servants who had drawn the water knew.
Then he called the bridegroom aside
¹⁰ *and said: "Everyone serves the good wine first and then*
the inferior wine after the guests have had too much to drink;
but you have saved the best till now."
¹¹ *What Jesus did here in Cana of Galilee was the first*
of the signs through which he revealed his glory;
and his disciples believed in him.

In this reading, Jesus reveals that the glory of God has indeed come. The glory is imaged in the wedding scene; but what is really being revealed is that Jesus has the power to change something very ordinary into something very special . He changes the water into wine, but, not just any wine, the best wine.

Reflect on this for a moment. We often hear people calling their spouse "their better half". When someone trusts another person and entrusts their life to that other person, they change. They offer themselves, they offer to care for the other person, to share with them. They think of the other before they think of themselves. They are transformed. In this reading, Jesus has shown that he can and does change things. Imagine how we can change if we allow him to change us!

Mary, his mother, trusts Jesus to do something when she sees there is a problem. Notice, she does not nag him or tell him what to do. She simply tells him that there is a problem and she trusts him to do something about it. Some say that in this story, she is a symbol of the faithful. She had faith in him and Jesus responded. There are at least two lessons to be learned here:

Reflect:

on times in your life
when someone or
something has changed
you in a good way.
Who were they? What
did they do or say that
changed you?
Thank God for helping
you through them.

1. By showing that he could change things, Jesus was preparing the disciples to believe that he would change the bread and wine into his Body and Blood so that he would remain with us always;
2. When we ask Jesus for something in faith, he responds to us.

The Catechism

This Gospel reveals to us how Mary prays and intercedes in faith. At Cana, Mary asks for the needs of the couple at the wedding feast (CCC 2618). We ask Mary to intercede for us too in our prayers. The Catechism also tells us that Christ is "really" present in the Eucharistic species: body and blood, soul and divinity (CCC 1374).

By way of preparing yourself for this session, consider the symbolism of the offering of the gifts. God gives us the rain, the sun and the earth, the grain and the grapes. We take them and make them into bread and wine and we offer them to him in the Eucharist. He then takes them and makes (changes) them into the Body and Blood of Christ. Likewise, we offer ourselves along with the bread and wine and we, too, are transformed. Christ lives within us and we bring him to the people we meet.

Leading the session

Welcome

As always, the session begins with the welcome of each person by name, saying something like: "Welcome [name]. It is good to see you today!" In this session, we will be seeing about how God can change things. You might show people the photo on the previous page or one of an offertory procession in their parish.

The human dimension
(the activity drawing on our life experience)

For this activity, we suggest you invite people to think about what happens at a wedding, and how getting married makes people change. You might try following this script (adapting it as you need to meet the abilities of the participants). If you don't think this would work, and you have access to a computer, you might use one of the wedding games where you dress the bride and groom and have a wedding, or you might make paper cut-outs to make the same point.

If you are going to act out a wedding, you will need: a bride and a bridegroom, a priest, and two witnesses. If you have a large group, use your imagination and get some people to be bridesmaids and ushers and others to be the congregation. You might want the bride and groom to dress up. You might also have multi-sensory items associated with wedding celebrations, such as bubbles, musical cards, glitter balls, to help to engage participants. Dress your meeting place up for the wedding (so that you can use it afterwards for the celebration).

Priest:	We are gathered here today to celebrate the marriage of this bride and groom [or use their names]. This is an important celebration. Two people will become one couple when they are married.
Priest:	Bride and groom: "Please join hands" Speaking to the groom: "Do you want to be married to this woman?"
Groom:	"I do".
Priest	Speaking to the bride: "Do you want to married to this man?"
Bride:	"I do".
Priest:	Speaking to the groom: "Will you give the bride a ring as a symbol of your love for her?"
Groom:	Placing the ring on the bride's finger: "Take this ring and remember I promise to love you forever".
Priest:	Speaking to the bride: "Will you give the groom a ring as a symbol of your love for him?"
Bride:	Placing the ring on the groom's finger: "Take this ring and remember that I promise to love you forever".
Priest:	I now pronounce you husband and wife. God has joined you together and nobody should separate you.

Moving to the special place

Get people to bring the flowers and other symbols you used for your "wedding" and add them to the focal point as your symbol of the wedding. If possible, add an earthenware jug to the focal point.

The religious dimension
(in the special place where Jesus speaks to us)

Lighting the candle

Once people have settled and are quiet, light the candle to remind us that Jesus is with us. Remember, he likes a good celebration!

Greeting the scripture

Linda Stassen's "Sing alleluia to the Lord"; is suitable for a wedding

> "Sing alleluia to the Lord. Sing alleluia to the Lord.
> Sing alleluia to the Lord. Sing alleluia, sing alleluia, sing alleluia."

Sign our heads, mouths and hearts

Ask someone in the group to explain why we do this.

Listening to Jesus in the scripture

Holding the book, read the scripture clearly and reverently to the whole group using an adapted version of the Gospel of John 2:1-11.

One day, there was a wedding at Cana in Galilee and Jesus,
his mother and his disciples were invited.
There were lots of people there and the wine ran out!
Jesus' mother noticed and she told him:
"They've run out of wine." Jesus paused for a moment and then he said:
"Why are you telling me? It isn't time for people to know
who I am." But she went to the servants
anyway and told them to do whatever Jesus said.
After a little while, Jesus went and told them to fill the jugs with water.
After that, he told them to take some of it to the waiter in charge
of the celebration. When the man had tasted it, he was surprised.
It was no longer water, but a very fine wine.
The Master called the bridegroom and said to him:
"Why have you kept the best wine until last?"
But the bridegroom had no idea what he was talking about.

Only the servants knew. And this was Jesus' first miracle.
Because of it, his disciples believed in him.

Giving the scripture message to each person

Now approach each member of the group individually, holding their hands and looking into their eyes, saying:

> "[Name] Jesus tells you today: I can change you if you want me to
> just like I changed the water in to wine and just like
> I change the bread and wine into my Body and Blood in Communion."

Reading the scripture again to the whole group

after each person has heard Jesus speaking to them.

Breaking the scripture open

You might like to use the Johnny Cash song, "He turned the water into wine" to open the scripture. It is a catchy, repetitive song. It is the kind of song that could invite percussion instruments in accompaniment.

Earlier in the session, we talked about how we offer ourselves to one another when we get married. We change as a result. In the Gospel, we heard about how Jesus turned water into wine. In the Mass, we offer bread and wine to Jesus and he changes them into his Body and Blood. It's not an easy concept to understand; it is one that is at the heart of our faith. Some people find it helpful to hear about how the caterpillar changes into a butterfly. It is still the same "being"; but it's outward appearance is completely changed. In exactly the opposite way, the bread and wine become the Body and Blood of Jesus. Their outward appearance remains the same; the bread still tastes like bread and the wine still tastes like wine, but we believe that they are changed into Jesus.

Seeing what Jesus did at Cana that day helped the disciples believe Jesus when he said he would change the bread and wine into his Body and Blood. By reflecting on this story, we, too, are helped to believe.

Getting the message

Give people time to hear Jesus what is saying to them today. On this occasion, consider finishing here with Graham Kendrick's song "Jesus put this song into my heart". It's a catchy tune reminiscent of a Jewish wedding song and people may well like to dance their way to where they will celebrate.

Sharing the message/celebrating

It's time to celebrate; to share the Good News with one another. If you acted out a wedding and created a wedding scene in your meeting place, you might return there for your sharing/celebration. You might make the sharing of food like a little buffet, wedding style, including even a pretend wedding cake. Make it fun; that makes it easier for people to open up to one another and share. Depending on your group, you might have a jug of water and some blackcurrant juice, and you can change the water into something more interesting and tasty to drink. Make the point that, of course, that is not what Jesus did. That's not the way to make wine! But it may add a little fun to the celebration. As a memento of the session, let them take some small pieces of cake home to their families (or the people in their care homes) like you would do from a wedding. Make sure they invite Jesus to the celebration. We know he loves a celebration and he likes to be invited to be with us. Encourage people to share what they liked best in this session. Ask them what they think about Jesus coming to us in bread and wine.

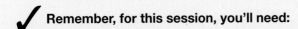

✓ Remember, for this session, you'll need:

✓ To introduce the session:
A photo of the offertory procession and gifts (in their parish if possible).

✓ Activity and special place:
A variety of multi-sensory items associated with wedding celebrations such as: veils, tiaras, a First Communion dress (if there are children) and a wedding dress (if there are adults), special suits (or bow ties) for the boys/men, a bouquet, musical wedding cards, mini-glitter balls, dress up props, such as hats for the girls/women, or wedding themed balloons. [Important note: Do what you can with what you have and with imagination; do not spend hours or money treating this like a shopping list.]

✓ Special place:
Your focal point may carry out the wedding theme with white or sparkly fabric and an earthenware jug and some plastic goblets. It would be good to have percussion instruments for the song "He turned the water into wine". As usual, you will need a candle that you can light, a draped cloth the holy book with the simplified reading placed inside. If you are going to have a wedding feast, you might have a wedding cake of sorts.

✓ Music:
All of these suggestions can be found on YouTube with visuals:
• Linda Stassen's "Sing alleluia to the Lord".
• Johnny Cash singing "He turned the water into wine".
• Graham Kendrick's song "Jesus put a song into my heart" which you can use to get people to dance their way from the special place to the celebration.

14. The Mass: We take and eat (the communion rite)

Session aim To hear Jesus tell us that he feeds us with his love so that our faith can grow, just like ordinary food helps our bodies to grow.

Preparing for the session

In this session we will hear Jesus telling us that he wants to feed us with his love so that we can become more like him. Our scripture for this session is the feeding of the five thousand. This story appears in all four Gospels (Mark 6:30-44, Luke 9:10-17, John 6:1-14 and Matthew 14:13-21). We will be using the Gospel of John. Most of us are familiar with having to make food go just a little further when an unexpected guest arrives and we have to share what we anticipated having with more people. Try to imagine what it must have been like for the disciples on that day, though, when Jesus fed five thousand with just a few loaves and fishes.

Read John 6:1-11

1 *After this, Jesus went to the other side*
   of the Sea of Galilee, also called the Sea of Tiberias.
2 *A large crowd kept following him,*
   because they saw the signs that he was doing for the sick.
3 *Jesus went up the mountain and sat down there with his disciples.*
4 *Now the Passover, the festival of the Jews, was near.*
5 *When he looked up and saw a large crowd coming toward him,*
   Jesus said to Philip: "Where are we to buy bread for these people to eat?"
6 *He said this to test him, for he himself*
   knew what he was going to do.
7 *Philip answered him: "Six months' wages would not buy*
   enough bread for each of them to get a little."
8 *One of his disciples, Andrew, Simon Peter's brother, said to him:*
9 *"There is a boy here who has five barley loaves and two fish.*
   But what are they among so many people?"
10 *Jesus said: "Make the people sit down."*
   Now there was a great deal of grass in the place;

Consider praying with this Gospel. Find a quiet place to sit and read the story. Then, imagine being at the scene with the disciples and the people. Just allow yourself to enter into the scene, to feel what it would have been like. You might be an onlooker—or you may want to be one of the disciples, one of the people, or the young man who was willing to share what he had. Thank God for the times when someone has shared something with you. Think about the times when you discovered that you had much more to give than you thought when you were willing to share with someone in need.

so they sat down, about five thousand in all.
[11] *Then, Jesus took the loaves, and, when he had given thanks,*
He distributed them to those who were seated;
so also the fish, as much as they wanted.

In the story of the feeding of the five thousand, Jesus is portrayed as showing concern for people's physical needs. He felt sorry for them. This story is important for our understanding of giving to the poor. Jesus gives the food to the disciples who are told to give it to the people. As followers of Jesus, we have a responsibility to the poor and for issues of world poverty.

There are a couple of other ways you might want to interpret this story in this session. One of them is about sharing. It is possible that when one person, who had food, was willing to share it with someone else, others got their food out and they, too, began to share it with those who didn't have food of their own. The miracle was in the fact that they changed from wanting to keep what they had for themselves to wanting or willing to share it and, in the end, there was enough for everyone.

You may also want to reflect on how this passage was another forerunner to the Last Supper and the Eucharist. Jesus gives himself as food to people in the Eucharist just as he gave the people food in the feeding of the five thousand. Listen to the words used by Jesus in these Gospels:

In Matthew's Gospel, we read:

"Taking the five loaves and the two fish,
he looked up to heaven,
and blessed and broke the loaves,
and gave them to the disciples,
and the disciples gave them to the crowds."
(Matthew 14:19)

At the Last Supper, we read:

"While they were eating, Jesus took a loaf of bread,
and after blessing it, he broke it, gave it to them."
(Mark 14:22)

In the Mass, we hear:

"Take this, all of you, and eat of it:
for this is my Body which will be given up for you "
(Eucharistic Prayer II)

By way of preparing yourself for this session, spend some time reflecting on how Jesus was able to turn water into wine at the wedding at Cana. Reflect on how Jesus was able to feed five thousand people from five loaves and two fishes. Does this help you believe that he can change the bread and wine into his Body and Blood? Does it help you believe that he can change you if you are willing to let him?

The Catechism

What ordinary food produces in our bodily life, Holy Communion achieves in our spiritual life. Our growth in Christian life needs the nourishment of Holy Communion (CCC 1392). Lastly, we have heard several times now how Christ is truly present in the Eucharist. He is present in the people who gather in his name and in the minister who presides at the Mass. He is present in the Word since it is he himself who speaks when the holy scriptures are read in the church, but most especially in the Eucharistic species (CCC 1088).

Leading the session

Welcome

Every session begins with the welcome of each person by name. In this session, we remember how, sometimes when we have visitors we were not expecting, we have had to share our cake with them, and one cake that would be cut into 8 pieces might have to be cut into smaller pieces to give the visitors each a piece of cake. You might bring a cake to the session that you can share afterwards (or show people a picture of one) and say that out of this cake, you could get eight big slices or 16 smaller slices of cake, if you are willing to share it with more people.

The human dimension
(the activity drawing on our life experience)

In this session, we suggest that you distribute the ingredients of tuna fish sandwiches

Note:

Ensure that care is taken before you offer or share food to ensure that people do not have any food allergies. At the beginning of your programme, it is important to ask participants, their parents or carers for permission to give people food and to inform you of any allergies.

to the participants. You will need a tin (or two) of tuna fish, perhaps some celery, mayonnaise, lettuce, bread and butter. Ask them how they might go about making the sandwiches. Hopefully, they will tell you that they will need to share their ingredients with the others in order to make the sandwiches. It doesn't have to be tuna fish sandwiches, although it's obvious why I suggested fish and bread. If you do choose something else, make sure it requires a few different ingredients in order to make the point that we have to share what we have to feed everyone.

Moving to the special place

The sandwiches or the cake can be the symbol for this session. Get people to carry it/them to the special place, and place them carefully on the focal point. You might also include some bread and a large host on the focal point. As you move to the special place, sing or listen to a bit of Dave Billbrough's "Let there be love".

> Let there be loved shared among us, let there be love in our eyes,
> let there be love shared among us, let there be love.

The religious dimension
(in the special place where Jesus speaks to us)

Lighting the candle

Once people have settled and are quiet, light the candle to remind us that Jesus is here.

Greeting the scripture

On this occasion, we suggest the chorus of Bob Hurd's, "In the breaking of the bread". The words work very well:

> "In the breaking of the bread, we have known him, we have been fed.
> Jesus the stranger, Jesus the Lord, be our companion; be our hope."

Sign our heads, mouths and hearts

Remind people why we sign our heads, our moths and our hearts.

Listening to Jesus in the scripture

Holding the book, read the scripture clearly and reverently to the whole group using an adapted version of the Gospel of John 6:1-11.

drawing by Kim Blundeel © 2014

One day Jesus went up a mountain with his disciples
but when the people heard it, they followed him
because he was healing the sick.
When he saw the big crowd Jesus asked: "Where can
we buy bread?" One of his disciples said:
"There is a boy here who has five loaves and two fish.
But it's not enough for so many people."
Jesus said: "Tell the people to sit on the grass."
Then, Jesus took the loaves, and,
when he had given thanks, he gave them to the disciples,
and the disciples gave them to the crowds.
And there was enough for everybody.

Giving the scripture message to each person

Now approach each member of the group individually, holding their hands and looking
into their eyes, saying:

> "[Name] Jesus tells you today, I am the bread of life and I am willing to share
> myself with you."

Reading the scripture to the whole group

After each person has heard Jesus speaking to them, the message is then given to the
whole group. You might ask people to imagine being part of the crowd and hearing Jesus
saying these words to them.

Breaking the scripture open

You might begin this part of the session with a song, perhaps Christopher Walker's "Jesus,
you are bread for us." The words are perfect for this session:

> Jesus, you are bread for us. Jesus, you are life for us.
> In your gift of Eucharist, we find love.
> When we feel we need a friend, You are there with us, Jesus.
> Thank you for the friend you are. Thank you for the love we share.

An alternative:

It works well if you animate the scripture by decorating some cut-out fish shapes so that at the right moment in the story/song they are brought out and collected up into 12 little baskets.
The activity of decorating the fish, throwing the fish out when the song is sung and then collecting them in the baskets can provide an accessible and enjoyable way of animating the scripture. Food sharing may be a preferred activity for this session for obvious reasons, but if some of the participants have medical conditions, this offers an alternative.

After they have had a chance to think about the words to the song they've listened to or sung, ask people to picture the scene of the Gospel story. (If they prefer, they can colour in the drawing above, which you will find on the additional resources CD). Imagine: they all ate the bread. Share the bread from the focal point.

We learn that when we give what we have to God, he can take it, bless it and do more than we could ever imagine. Even though we may not have very much, when we are willing to share, little becomes much when it is placed in God's hands. At Mass, we offer the bread and wine. The priest asks God to change it into Jesus. Then he gives us a small piece of the bread because Jesus wants to share himself with us. Jesus wants to feed us with his love. If you have a large host, break it and share it with everyone. (Explain that the host is not Jesus; it has not yet been changed.) Make the point that there is enough for everyone.

Getting the message

Give people time to hear Jesus is saying that to them today. They may not be able to articulate what they are thinking and feeling. Bring this part of the session to a close with some quiet music, possibly the Taizé chant (response only): "Eat this bread, drink this cup, come to me and never be hungry", or the refrain of John Foley's "One bread, one body".

You are now ready to move to the place where you will celebrate. If your activity at the beginning of the session was to make tuna fish sandwiches, remind them that we have brought our own bread and fish to our special place and invite them to take them to the place where they will celebrate.

photo by Diana Klein

150

Sharing the message/celebrating

It's time to celebrate; to share the cake and the tuna fish sandwiches with one another. You've been sharing and celebrating at the end of every session for a while now. You might ask them what sharing is like for them, and what it is like when others are willing to share with them. Remember how important this part of the session is. It is the time when friendships are developed, when people have fun, when they talk about what they have enjoyed about the session, but also what they enjoy about being together and doing things together. If you are sharing the sandwiches and the cake that you used during the session, arrange them on trays and get people to serve one another, emphasising the aspects of offering and sharing. You might also introduce the sharing by a short prayer before meals. This one can be downloaded free from the Widgit website:

| Bless us | O Lord | and | these | your | gifts | which | we | are | about to receive |

| from | your | bounty | through | Christ | our | Lord | Amen. |

✓ **Remember, for this session, you'll need:**

✓ **To introduce the session:**
A cake, if possible. Make it a size that people will be able to see what you are saying about being able to have a large piece each or, if everyone is to have a piece, they will only have a small piece.

✓ **Activity and special place:**
A tin or two of tuna fish and some bread which will be made into tuna fish sandwiches, mayonnaise (and perhaps celery and lettuce), French bread and a large unconsecrated host, As usual, you will also need the usual cloths for the focal point, an icon of Jesus or a crucifix, a candle, the holy book with the simplified reading placed inside.

✓ **Music: All of this music is available on YouTube:**
• Dave Billbrough's "Let there be love shared among us".
• Christopher Walker's "Jesus, you are bread for us".
• Taizé chant (response only): "Eat this bread, drink this cup, come to me and never be hungry".
• John Foley's "One bread, one body".
• Bob Hurd's "In the breaking of the bread".

Other useful resources:
See Henry Martin's *Presentation of the feeding of the 5,000* on Sermons4Kids which allows free use for ministry purposes (www.Sermons4kids.com).
Grace before meals: can be downloaded free and printed for each person (www.widgit.com).

15. The Mass: We go out (the dismissal rite)

Session aim

To understand that Jesus sends us out at the end of the Mass to be like him in the world, to bring his love to others.

Preparing for the session

Today we will be talking about what we are told to do when we leave Mass. In the new translation of the missal, one of the prayers of dismissal is to "go in peace, glorifying the Lord by your life". Jesus sends us out to bring his love to those we meet. By way of introducing this session, I suggest you reflect on the kind of experiences we all have of wanting to be like people we admire — and wanting to tell others about those people. You might think of a saint, a parent, a teacher, a famous actor or actress, or a sportsperson. I invite you to reflect on what it is like for you to be like Jesus, wanting to tell others about him.

Explore some of the ways people live by Jesus' law of love. Some ideas to consider:

- Being helpful to others; acts of kindness (sometimes random ones);
- Contributing to the charities who help the poor at home and in other parts of the world;
- Giving food to a food bank; helping in some way to feed the hungry;
- Visiting the sick and housebound, or calling to make contact;
- Praying for people who are sick or who are having problems;
- Forgiving others, however hard it may be.

Think about how you live by God's law of love, and what helps you to feel and know the love and friendship of Jesus. You might be surprised at how many examples you can think of.

Matthew 28:16-20

[16] *Now the eleven disciples went to Galilee,*
to the mountain to which Jesus had directed them.
[17] *When they saw him, they worshipped him; but some doubted.*

¹⁸ *And Jesus came and said to them:*
"All authority in heaven and on earth has been given to me.
¹⁹ *Go therefore, and make disciples of all nations,*
baptising them in the name of the Father
and of the Son and of the Holy Spirit,
²⁰ *and teaching them to obey everything*
that I have commanded you. And remember,
I am with you always, to the end of the age."

The focus of this Gospel is the experience of Jesus acting in our lives in various ways, even though we can't see him in the same way as the disciples did when he was on earth. This Gospel story takes place after Jesus' resurrection. The disciples thought they would never see Jesus again; but the angel appeared to the women at the tomb and told them that Jesus had risen and that the disciples should go meet him in Galilee. The Gospel tells us that when the disciples found Jesus there, he told them to make disciples of all nations, baptising them and teaching them to obey everything that he had commanded. He reminded them that he is with us always, even to the end of the time.

Consider what modern-day disciples are doing. Are they preaching, baptising and teaching? Consider the many ways the Church teaches. There are the obvious answers: religious education in our schools and catechetics in our parishes, sacramental preparation, scripture studies and other adult formation. What about the homily at Sunday Mass? This is a form of teaching too, helping us to break open the scriptures and act on them in our lives. In other words, there are innumerable modern-day disciples helping us to hear Jesus speaking to us today.

By way of preparing yourself for this session, spend some time reflecting on Jesus' last words in this Gospel: "Remember, I am with you always". How good it is to hear these words over and over again!

The Catechism

As a result of Jesus' visible presence being taken away from the disciples, their communion with him became more intense (CCC 788). The Catechism reminds us that as we believe that the risen Christ is with us always, it is always possible to pray, no matter what trouble may arise (CCC 1743).

Leading the session

Welcome

As always, the session begins with the welcome of each person by name, saying something like: "Welcome [name]. It is good to see you today!" This session, we are going to think about how we imitate people we admire. Ask people who they admire and what they might do to copy them. Ask them if they could choose to walk in a person's shoes, who would they choose?

The human dimension
(the activity drawing on our life experience)

You might have a selection of footwear: football boots, running shoes, wellington boots, ballet shoes, and so on. If it is practical, allow people to put the shoes on and to say who they are imitating. Explore some of the ways people they know live by Jesus' law of love. Some they may come up with:

- Being helpful, loving, caring to others;
- Being kind, willing to share;
- Giving food to the hungry;
- Visiting people who are sick and housebound;
- Praying for people who are sick or who are having problems;
- Forgiving others.

The "What's best in helping me feel and know the love and friendship of Jesus?" Widgit cards can be played to draw on people's life experience in this session. People are invited to respond to the question by choosing from a selection of cards, including (but certainly not limited) to the following ones. You will find all these cards on the additional resources CD, pages 38–39.

Then, invite people to choose from a selection of other cards to find answers; but don't stop them from giving other answers:

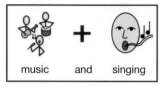  

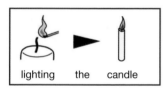  

These lotto exercises are fun; and they make learning accessible for people with learning disabilities, autism, downs syndrome or dyslexia. They help people for whom English is an additional language, people with severe physical difficulties, and so on.

Moving to the special place

In this session, we suggest the symbol you bring to your special place is the lotto card exercise. Make a procession from the meeting place to the special place and allow each person to place their card or cards on the focal point and then sit down. Take your time.

The religious dimension
(in the special place where Jesus speaks to us)

Lighting the candle

We light the candle to remind us that Jesus is the light in our lives, the one who guides and leads us to be like him. He is here with us.

Greeting the scripture

To greet the Gospel in this session, I suggest you sing the chorus of Robert Dufford's "Be Not Afraid".

> "Be not afraid. I go before you always; Come follow me, and I will give you rest."

Sign our heads, mouths and hearts

Remind people we do this because we hear God's word in our heads, proclaim it with our mouths and feel it in our hearts.

Listening to Jesus in the scripture

Holding the book, speak reverently and clearly and read the scripture to the whole group. We suggest using this simplified version of Gospel of Matthew 28:16-20.

The eleven disciples went to the mountain in Galilee
where Jesus asked them to meet him.
He told them: "All authority in heaven
and on earth has been given to me.
I am asking you to tell everyone about me,
to make them my followers,
to love them and baptise them in the name of
the Father and of the Son and of the Holy Spirit.
Teach people what I have taught you,
and remember, I am with you always to the end of time."

Giving the scripture message to each person

Now approach each member of the group individually, saying:

> "[Name] Jesus tells you today, Go out at the end of Mass;
> walk in my shoes and tell others about me."

Reading the scripture again to the whole group

After each person has heard Jesus speaking to them, the scripture message is then given to the whole group.

Breaking the scripture open

Jesus told the disciples to go tell everyone about him, to teach them what they had learned and to make disciples. All Christians are his disciples. Encourage people to think about who helps them to feel and know the love and friendship of Jesus; who helps them to know the love of God, the love of Jesus.

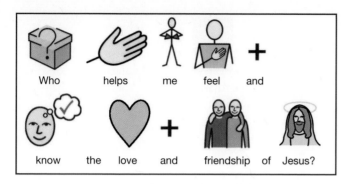

Give each person a copy of this question card. They can choose from the cards below, found on pages 28–29 of the additional resources CD. Remember this is the way to enable participation of people with learning disabilities in responding to the questions you pose.

Don't limit people if they want to suggest other people, for example, grandparents, crossing guards, bus drivers, kind neighbours, and so on. Ask them how they help others. People with learning disabilities are often very good at loving others by the unconditional love they offer others. Try to make the link between being loving and being Christ-like. Jesus wants us to walk in his shoes. What kind of things would this involve?

- Helping in a soup kitchen or charity event in their parish;
- Contributing used clothes to charity;
- Offering a friend or neighbour help with shopping or gardening;
- By being kind to people and animals, caring about others;
- By smiling at people, especially people who seem sad or lonely;
- Holding someone's hand if they are afraid.

Note:

You might extend the idea of choice to a cut and stick activity for those you think would enjoy it.

Getting the message

Give people time to hear Jesus is saying that to them today. Be aware that the scripture message and what people hear Jesus saying may not be one and the same; but ask them to think about ways they can walk in Jesus' shoes (or sandals). You might have a couple of pairs of sandals that they can put on as they imagine what they can do. The idea is to help them be aware that they can be like Jesus. Warning: if you are working with some autistic people, they may be confused by the idea of walking in Jesus' shoes literally so you may need to express this in a different way.

Close this part of the session

You might end this part of the session with the chorus to Alan Dale's hymn "God's spirit is in my heart", which makes the same points you've been making in the session.

Sharing the message/celebrating

It's time to celebrate; to share the Good News with one another. You might suggest that each person finds a partner and they tell one another all the things they do to be kind or helpful. Ask them whether they have ever thought they were being like Jesus when they did those things. Sharing food with one another during this part of the session is important. You might print some of the Widgit symbols on sticky labels and ask people to stick labels on one another to say what things they do that make them like Jesus. Remind people that Jesus likes a good party; we hear lots of stories about how he liked eating and sharing food with his friends. Remember, Jesus is still with us during this celebration, and this may actually be the time and place where they feel his presence most.

✓ **Remember, for this session, you'll need:**

✓ **To introduce the session:**
Ideas of people the group might imitate; Different kinds of footwear that the people the group admires might wear (football boots, running shoes, ballet shoes, wellington boots and so on).

✓ **Activity and special place:**
• Widgit cards to ask the question you want to ask and to offer a selection of responses. For more information about Widgit, visit: www.widgit.com.
• For the focal point, you will need the usual cloths, an icon of Jesus, a candle that you can light, the holy book with the simplified reading placed inside.

✓ **Music:**
• Robert Dufford's "Be Not Afraid (I Go Before You Always)" free MP3 download on http://www.hymnlyrics.org/requests/ be_not_ afraid_i_go_before_you_always.php.
• Alan Dale's hymn: "God's spirit is in my heart" — several YouTube versions available.

Preparing to celebrate the sacraments of initiation

Baptism, confirmation and the Eucharist

Note: The preparation for these three sacraments are being covered in separate sessions, although candidates might well celebrate all three sacraments simultaneously

Preparing to celebrate baptism

 Session aim To learn what happens at baptism. This session should be especially helpful for those preparing for baptism.

Preparing for the session

The baptismal liturgy, with its symbols of water, oil, light and white garment, recalls into the present the reality of Christ's redeeming work: his dying and rising; his ministry, and the meaning of this for us as members of his Church. Our very use of the word "baptism", which in Greek means "immersion", has become a metaphor for our belief that we, by dying in Christ, are immersed into the life of Christ, who is the resurrection and the life. This session will take the participants through a simplified baptism.

Mark 1:9-11

9 *In those days, Jesus came from Nazareth of Galilee*
and was baptised by John in the Jordan.
10 *And, just as he was coming up out of the water,*
He saw the heavens torn apart and the Spirit
descending like a dove on him.
11 *And a voice came from heaven:*
"You are my Son, the Beloved: with you I am well pleased."

In his baptism, Jesus embodies both sides of the promised relationship of love between God and his people. As God, he represents God to us. As human, he represents humanity to God. This relationship that God has created between himself and humanity in the person of Jesus Christ is the fulfilment of everything God promised to Israel, to the House of David, and through Israel to all of the world. In Christ, God has demonstrated in person his utter faithfulness to his covenant of love and redemption. God saves us because he loves us and wants us saved, and he did it in Jesus Christ.

The Catechism

Baptism is the gateway to life in the Spirit and the door which gives access to the other sacraments (CCC 1213). It is called a bath of enlightenment, because those who are baptised are enlightened in their understanding. Having received in baptism the

Word, the true light that enlightens every person, the one who is baptised has been "enlightened," he becomes a child of light.

St Gregory of Nazianzus said: "Baptism is God's most beautiful and magnificent gift… We call it gift, grace, anointing, enlightenment, garment of immortality, bath of rebirth, seal, and most precious gift. It is called gift because it is conferred on those who bring nothing of their own; grace, since it is given even to the guilty; baptism, because sin is buried in the water; anointing, for it is priestly and royal as are those who are anointed; enlightenment, because it radiates light; clothing, since it veils our shame; bath, because it washes; and seal, as it is our guard and the sign of God's Lordship."

By way of preparing yourself for this session, hear God calling you his beloved and telling you that in you he is well pleased. Sit with those words and feel their power. Know just how profound these words can be for the one who hears them.

Some advice for this session

The aim of this session is to help people get a sense of the importance of being baptised. Show the participants the Widgit cards and talk to them in the place where you gather. Make sure you have a set of cards for each person. Ask people to place their cards on a tray (or a box top) with the template of the church in it as you go through the rite of baptism.

Keep this session simple:

Before you begin, establish who the parents will be, who the godparents will be and who will be baptised. You might choose one of the group who is being prepared for baptism

Widgit cards:

You will find a basic set of baptism Widgit cards on page 29, additional resources CD. If you want an extensive set of symbols, you will find it in the ICYF 2 pack for a small fee (http://www. widgit.com/resources/ curriculum/re/i_call_you_ friends/index.htm).

Photo: Diana Klein

A child waits in anticipation of her baptism

(or you might choose to use a doll). Gather in the porch or narthex of the church and welcome people as usual by name. Have someone ready to offer people a booklet or the Widgit cards in lieu of a hymn book. If you are using Widgit cards, you will probably need the cards below.

Encourage people to greet each other, to welcome one another and take the widgit priest and put him in the sanctuary.

Priest:	"Welcome, everyone to the baptism of this child (or person)."
(To the parents, he says:)	"What's the baby's name?" or, "What is your name?" (if the person being baptised is not a baby).
Priest:	(Asks the parents or the person being baptised:) "What are you asking for?"
The parents:	"Baptism."

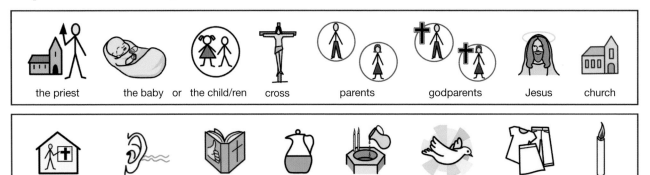

the priest   the baby   or   the child/ren   cross   parents   godparents   Jesus   church

catechist   listen   holy book   oil   baptism   Holy Spirit   white garment   candle

Baptism area in the parish of Sacred Heart and Mary Immaculate, Mill Hill

© John Green

162

Priest:	"[Name of the baby or person being baptised], the Christian community welcomes you with great joy. I am now going to mark you with a cross on your forehead as a sign that you belong to Jesus."
The Priest:	"Do you want your child to become a member of the Christian family, to belong to Jesus?"
The parents:	"Yes." Or, if the one being baptised is not a baby, he asks: "Do you want to become a member of the Christian family, to belong to Jesus?" and they answer "Yes."
The Priest:	(To the parents if it is a child being baptised:) "It will be your job to teach your child to know Jesus and bring him or her to church. Will you do that?"
The parents:	"Yes."
Priest (to the godparents:)	"Are you willing to help these parents in this important job?"
The godparents:	"Yes, we are."

Everyone sits down and listens to the Gospel.

Greeting the Gospel

We greet the Gospel with the refrain from "Up from the waters into life" by Marty Haughen.

Sign our heads, mouths and hearts

Listening to Jesus in the scripture

The priest reads this or another simplified version of the Gospel of Mark 1:9-11

Jesus came from Nazareth of Galilee
and was baptised by John in the Jordan.
He went right down under the water.
As he was coming out of the river, he looked up.
A strong wind was blowing and he felt
the Holy Spirit descending like a dove on him.
And a voice came from heaven saying:
"You are my Son, I love you and
I am very pleased with you."

ICYF 2 pack has a lotto game for this scripture for a small fee (http://www.widgit.com/resources/curriculum/re/i_call_you_friends/index.htm).

Giving the scripture message to each person

The priest or the leader goes to each person, and, holding their hands and looking into their eyes says:
"[Name] Jesus says to you today:
I love you and I am very pleased with you."

Breaking the scripture open

The priest or the leader with break the scripture open and help people get the message. He might ask people to think about how good it feels when someone tells you that they love you and that they are pleased with you. The great thing about God is that he always loves us. There is nothing that will stop him from loving us.

The priest then puts a touch of oil on the child's breast and says: "May Jesus give you strength." Then, blessing the water by making a sign of the cross over it, the priest says: "Bless this water. It will be used for this baptism."

Turning to all present, the priest says: "Do you believe what the Church teaches? Do you believe in God the Creator?" All respond: "Yes, we do."

"And do you believe in Jesus, his son, who died on the cross and came alive again?" All say: "Yes, we do."

"And, do you believe in the Holy Spirit, who guides and inspires us?" All respond: "Yes, we do."

The priest says to the parents: "Do you want your child to believe these things?" or he asks the older child or adult being baptised: "Do you believe these things?" and they say "yes".

The priest then says to the godparents: "Do you promise to make sure to help to teach him/her about Jesus?" and the godparents say: "Yes."

The priest then pours water over the baby or person's head and says: "I baptise you in the name of the Father, and of the Son and of the Holy Spirit." All respond: "Amen."

The priest uses the oil to make the sign of the cross on the child or person's head and says: "May you live like Jesus."

When we are anointed with the oil of chrism, we are made Christ-like, we are given a share in the priestly, prophetic and royal ministry of Jesus. That carries the expectation that we will proclaim God's word, we will tell people what God is like and we will care for one another.

The priest places the white blanket on the person or the child, with the parents' and godparents' help, and says: "Receive this white garment. It is a sign that you will live forever."

The white garment is a sign of being a new Christian; but it is more than that. It is the uniform of heaven. We share in eternal life now through our baptism.

The candle is lit and it is handed to the child or person (or held for them) and the priest says: "Receive the light of Christ. Parents/godparents, God has given you the job of keeping this light alive. May God bless this newly baptised child/person and may they walk in the light always."

Play some inspiring music. You might use Michael Joncas' "On eagle's wings". If people want to join in with the music, let them. If they want to dance, encourage them.

> You who dwell in the shelter of the Lord
> Who abide in his shelter for life.
> Say to the Lord, my refuge, my rock in whom I trust
>
> *Chorus: And he will raise you up on eagle's wings*
> *Bear you on the breath of dawn*
> *Make you to shine like the sun*
> *And hold you in the palm of his hand.*
>
> The snare of the fowler will never get you down
> and famine will bring you no fear.
> Under your wings your refuge
> his faithfulness your shield. *Chorus*
>
> And for to his angels he's given a command
> to guard you in all of your ways.
> Upon their hands they will bear you up
> lest you dash your foot against a stone. *Chorus*

Alternative song:

There is a really good celebratory song that would work here with percussion and dance. "When the spirit of the Lord is within my heart I will dance like David danced" by Benny Hinn. You can also change the name for the names of those participating.

Getting the message

Before you go to the place where you will celebrate, you might ask everyone to take a moment to hear God saying to them: "[Name: You are mine and I love you." Be aware that not everyone will be getting the same message.

Sharing the message/celebrating

Everyone now goes to the place where you will celebrate and have a baptism party. Everyone can be invited: grandparents, brothers and sisters and all the family, aunts, uncles, cousins and neighbours. There will be a special baptism cake for everyone to share and it will be a very good celebration. Special events in our lives are marked with celebrations like this because we want to remember the occasion. Ask people to bring something for the celebration, something they want to contribute; and as they present their contribution, get them to say why they chose to bring what they did. Ask what they have learned about celebrations.

 Remember, for this session, you'll need:

 Activity:
- To have invited the priest to help with the session;
- The Widgit lotto pieces. Sheets containing basic images are available on the additional resources CD; ICYF 2 offers an extensive set of cards to take people through the rite of baptism for a small fee (http://www.widgit.com/resources/curriculum/re/i_call_you_friends/index.htm);
- To have a catechist or parent for each member of the group to help them go through the baptism with the symbols;
- A candle, the holy book with the simplified reading placed inside;
- A baptism cake, balloons and drinks for the celebration.

✓ **Music: all available on YouTube:**
- "Up from the waters into life" by Marty Haughen;
- "On eagle's wings" based on Psalm 91 by Michael Joncas (chords and music available on http://tabs.ultimate-guitar.com/h/hymnal/on_eagles_wings_crd.htm;
- "When the Spirit of the Lord is within my heart, I will dance like David danced" by Benny Hinn;
- Stephen Dean's, blessing of water: "Water of life" refrain could be sung repeatedly: Waters of life, cleanse and refresh us; raise us to life in Christ Jesus;
- Michael Saward's "Baptised in water". There are three verses; but you can use just the third verse and repeat it. It is sung to the melody of "Morning has broken":
  Baptised in water, sealed by the Spirit,
  marked with the sign of Christ our King:
  born of one Father, we are his children,
  joyfully now God's praises we sing.
- Daniel Shutte's "Yahweh, I know you are near" is also beautiful and suitable.

Preparing to celebrate confirmation

 Session aim To learn that we are anointed with holy oil to heal and protect us, and to strengthen us spiritually.

Preparing for the session

The session will help people understand what happens when we celebrate the sacrament of confirmation. It can be used for a practice if there are people in the group who are being confirmed, or it can be used simply to help people get a glimpse at yet another sacrament where God communicates his unconditional love to us.

John 16:4. 7. 13

4 *Jesus said: "I have said these things to you so that when their*
 hour comes you may remember what I told you about them.
 I did not say these things to you from the beginning
 because I was with you.
7 *Nevertheless, I tell you the truth:*
 it is to your advantage that I go away,
 for if I do not go away, the Advocate will not come to you.
13 *When the Spirit of truth comes, he will guide you*
 into all the truth; for he will not speak on his own,
 but will speak whatever he hears,
 and he will declare to you the things that are to come.

Jesus is speaking of the Advocate he will send his disciples, the Spirit of truth who comes from the Father. He will defend them against the disbelieving world and guide them into the truth. The Advocate will show Jesus' disciples how wrong the world is in their understanding of sin, justice and judgement. He tells them that the Spirit will guide them into the way of truth Jesus revealed to them, and will lead them to a fuller understanding of what they heard from Jesus. They will not be left on their own.

The Catechism

The eternal origin of the Holy Spirit is revealed in his mission in time. The Spirit is sent to the apostles and to the Church both by the Father in the name of the Son, and by the Son in person, once he had returned to the Father.

The sending of the person of the Spirit after Jesus' glorification reveals in its fullness the mystery of the Holy Trinity. (CCC244)

By way of preparing yourself for this session take some time to think about what confirmation means to you and ask yourself what part the Holy Spirit plays in your life.

Leading the session

Welcome

In this session, you might say: "Jesus welcomes you today [name]. We are going to learn about what happens during a confirmation. If you are going to be confirmed, this will help you to prepare. If you are already confirmed, you might find it a good reminder about what happened at your confirmation and how you experience the presence of the Holy Spirit in your life."

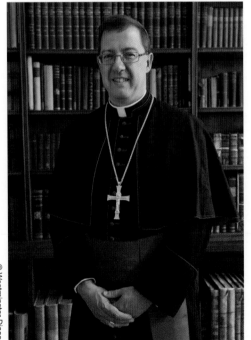

Bishop John Sherrington, Auxiliary Bishop in Westminster

© Westminster Diocese

The human dimension
(the activity drawing on our life experience)

Meet in your usual place outside the church and have a focal point of a table set with a red/orange table cloth, some oil in a special container with a strong perfume in it, or some other strongly scented ointment used for healing, such as Deep Heat or Mint Ease. You might also have a photo of the bishop who normally comes for confirmations (or the one you know will be coming if this is a practice for a confirmation you will shortly be celebrating).

Ask if anyone has ever hurt themselves in some way and experienced an ache afterwards. If they haven't had that kind of experience, they might be aware of friends or family or sportspeople who have, or they may have seen adverts on TV for ointments that will help people with aches and pains. The ointment heals and protects, it strengthens our bodies. Allow people to take some of the ointment and rub it on their arms. Invite them to see how it disappears into us, even though the smell of it remains for a little while.

Then show them the holy oil, which also has a scent. Talk about how the bishop anoints us with holy oil when we are confirmed. It heals and protects; it strengthens us spiritually.

Moving to the special place

Once again, keep this session simple:

- Move from your meeting place into the church;
- When they go into the church, invite people to bless themselves with holy water and tell them that, when they do this, they are reminding themselves that they are baptised people. Since confirmation confirms and strengthens baptism, this is an important link to make;
- Ask them to genuflect (or bow if they are unable to genuflect);
- Ask the priest to come into the church and go to the altar to welcome everyone and explain that the bishop comes to confirm people; and, when he does, this happens:
- The Mass begins as it usually does.
- When it is time for the Gospel, the priest will go to the lectern. Ask him to read this simplified version of John 16: 4. 7. 13. Follow the usual pattern of your sessions.

Greeting the Gospel

Sign our heads, our mouths and our hearts.

Listening to Jesus in the Gospel

Jesus said: "I am going to leave you soon,
for I am going back to my Father.
But I will not leave you alone, I will send someone to help you.
You will not be able to see me,
but you will have my Holy Spirit to help you and guide you."

- Immediately after he reads the gospel, the candidates will be called by name: As their name is called, the candidate should stand up (if they can) and answer: "Here I am". (If any of the candidates cannot stand up, remember to explain that to the priest (and the bishop on the day of confirmation).
- The priest will speak very briefly, repeating that Jesus has said to each and every person: Jesus says to you [Name]: "I am going to leave you
and go back to my Father in heaven; but I will not leave you alone.
I will send my Holy Spirit to help you and guide you."

- The bishop will give a homily. Shortly after he became the Holy Father, Pope Francis invited young people from all over the world to Rome and he confirmed them in St Peter's Square. He told them that the "new things of God are not like the novelties of this world — all of which are temporary; they come and they go and we keep looking for more."

  "The new things which God gives to our lives are lasting," he continued, "not only in the future, when we will be with him, but today as well. God is even now making all things new; the Holy Spirit is truly transforming us, and through us he also wants to transform the world in which we live." He invited people to "open the doors to the Spirit, let ourselves be guided by the Spirit and allow God's constant help to make us new people, inspired by the love of God which the Holy Spirit bestows on us!"

  Most important, the Pope said how beautiful it would be if each of us, every evening, could say: "Today at school, at home, at work, guided by God, I showed a sign of love towards one of my friends, my parents, an older person!" (Pope Francis, homily, Confirmation Mass in St Peter's Square, 28 April 2013)

  In these materials, we have talked about offering ourselves to God, knowing that the Spirit can and will transform us if we are willing. We talked about the Gifts of the Spirit and how we use them for the service of others. What a good idea to ask ourselves when we say our night-time prayers, just how we have showed a sign of love towards one of our friends, our parents or an older person.

- The priest will explain to the candidates that they will be asked to renew their baptismal promises. I suggest that you keep them simple and use the same ones we used in the sessions on baptism. You will have to decide if you should use the fuller version.

  "Do you believe in God the Creator?"
  All respond: "Yes, we do."
  "And do you believe in Jesus, his son, who died on the cross and came alive again?"
  All respond: "Yes, we do."
  "And, do you believe in the Holy Spirit, who guides and inspires us?"
  All respond: "Yes, we do."

The bishop will then say a special prayer for those being confirmed.

In baptism, God, our Father gave new birth of eternal life
to his chosen sons and daughters.
Let us pray to our Father that he will pour out the Holy Spirit
to strengthen his sons and daughters with his gifts and anoint them
to be more like Christ, the Son of God.
All-powerful God, Father of our Lord Jesus Christ, by water and the Holy Spirit,
you freed your sons and daughters
from sin and gave them new life. Send
your Holy Spirit upon them to be their
helper and guide.
Give them the spirit of wisdom and
understanding,
the spirit of right judgement and
courage,
the spirit of knowledge and reverence.
Fill them with the spirit of wonder and
awe in your presence.
We ask this through Christ our Lord.
All respond: Amen.

If you need to simplify it, try this:

In baptism, God, our Father chose us
to be his sons and daughters.
Let us pray to our Father
that he will pour out the Holy Spirit
on you to strengthen you with his gifts
and anoint you to be more like Jesus.
All-powerful God, send your
Holy Spirit upon these people
to be their helper and guide.
Give them the spirit of
wisdom and understanding,
the spirit of right judgement
and courage,

Cardinal Vincent Nichols
confirming Raphael Maffeo
at Sacred Heart and Mary
Immaculate Parish in 1996, in
Mill Hill in north London when
the cardinal was an auxiliiary
in Westminster

Photo: Diana Klein

the spirit of knowledge and reverence.
Fill them with the spirit of wonder
and awe in your presence.
We ask this through Christ our Lord.
All respond: Amen.

The bishop will then lay hands on each of the candidates. Ask them to imagine God reaching through the clouds and touching their heads. Each person to be confirmed goes to the bishop with his or her sponsor. They bow together to the bishop. The candidate then stands or kneels in front of the bishop and the sponsor places his or her right hand on the candidate's left shoulder.

The bishop dips his right thumb in the holy oil and makes the sign of the cross on the forehead of the one to be confirmed, as he says:

"[Name] be sealed with the Gift of the Holy Spirit."

The newly confirmed replies: "Amen".
The bishop then says: "Peace be with you".
And the newly confirmed replies: "And with your spirit."

Choosing a confirmation name

If it is the tradition for people to choose a confirmation name, the bishop will address them by this name. Consider how you will help them to choose. You may find the ICYF/

Bishop Alan Hopes, Bishop of East Anglia in 2006 for confirmations in Teddington when he was Auxilliary Bishop in Westminster

Photo: Diana Klein

Come and See pack 2 helpful. It contains a range of boys and girls symbol supported text stories of saints to help people make their choice. See http://www.widgit.com/resources/curriculum/re/i_call_you_friends/index.htm. A small fee applies.

Getting the message

Remember to give people time to hear Jesus is speaking to them today and how the Spirit will touch them when they are confirmed.

Close this part of the session

The Mass then continues as usual. Bring this part of the session to a close with some quiet music, or perhaps Daniel Iverson's hymn, "Spirit of the living God". You are now ready to move to where you will celebrate.

Sharing the message and celebrating

It is time to have refreshments, where people can share with one another what this time together has been like for them. If they are preparing to be confirmed, offer any reassurance they need if they are anxious in any way. Join in their joy if they are excited and answer any questions they may have.

 Remember, for this session, you'll need:

 To introduce the session:
- Oil in a special container of some kind with a strong perfume in it;
- Some other ointment used for healing which has a strong scent, such as, Deep Heat or Mint Ease.
- You might also have a photo of the bishop who normally comes for confirmations.

✓ **Activity and special place:**
- To organise the priest to be present and the church to be available;
- A table with an orange/red table cloth, with:
- The holy book with the simplified reading placed inside, a candle, a crucifix or an icon;
- Either the chrism oil or some other oil in a special container;
- A copy of the baptismal promises.

 Music:
You might use this as an opportunity to introduce the music that will be used at the confirmation Masses. Some ideas:
- "Spirit of the living God" Daniel Iverson;
- "Gather your people, O Lord" by Bob Hurd based on 1 Cor 12, Is 2:3-4, 11:9;
- "The love I have for you, my Lord" by Carey Landry;
- "Shine, Jesus, shine" by Graham Kendrick;
- "This is the day" by Les Garrett.

Preparing to receive Holy Communion

 Session aim — To learn or be reminded how to approach and receive Holy Communion.

Preparing for the session

In this session, you will be preparing (or reminding) people how to receive Holy Communion. If people are given communion under both kinds, they should be offered it that way in this session. For people who are going to receive their First Holy Communion, this will be a very important session. People who are already receiving communion might find this session a good reminder about how to do so.

1 Corinthians 11:23-25

²³ *For I have received from the Lord what I also handed on to you,*
 that the Lord Jesus on the night when he was betrayed took a loaf of bread,
²⁴ *and when he had given thanks, he broke it and said:*
 "This is my body that is for you. Do this in remembrance of me."
²⁵ *In the same way he took the cup also after supper, saying:*
 "This cup is the new covenant in my blood.
 Do this, as often as you drink it, in remembrance of me."

Important note:

When the Jews talk about blood, they are referring to life; whereas, we often associate blood with death. Some people (especially autistic people who hear things in a very literal way) find this explanation helpful.

Jesus took an existing feast, the most important of the Jewish celebrations and changed it into something new. Throughout the Old Testament, God is constantly renewing the covenant made with human beings. In the book of Jeremiah, God promises a new covenant, not like the previous one, saying that he would put his law within them. He said he would write it upon their hearts and would be their God. He said he would forgive them and forget their sins (Jeremiah 31:31-34). This new covenant was brought about at the Last Supper when Jesus offered his life, present in the bread and in the wine.

The Catechism

The main thing to stress when talking about the Eucharist is that the whole point of it is love. John says "God is love" and Jesus is the perfect sacrament, or sign, of the love of God. We receive this love in the Eucharist. God is love, Jesus is love, we receive love, we become love. Just as our everyday diet affects our health, our behaviour, who we are, what we become, so this spiritual food affects our spiritual life (CCC 1362-1368 the Eucharist: memorial, past made present).

By way of preparing yourself for this session, reflect on what happens when you receive Holy Communion. How do you prepare yourself spiritually?

Leading the session

Welcome

As always, the session begins with the welcome of each person by name, saying something like: "Welcome [name]. It is good to see you today!" In this session, "Jesus welcomes you today [name]. We are going to learn how to approach Jesus and receive Holy Communion." You will have the opportunity of receiving a host and some wine. It has not been consecrated, so it is not yet Jesus. It is still bread and wine and it will help you practise how to receive Jesus properly.

The human dimension
(the activity drawing on our life experience)

Meet in your usual meeting place and have a focal point of a table set with a plate, a napkin, a goblet, a candle, flowers, and a small loaf of sliced bread (or a piece of pitta bread) and some juice. (Depending on your group, you might ask them to set the table.) You might ask people if the table looks like it is set for a very special meal. Explain that your session today will help them learn how the Mass is a special meal too. Show people the loaf of bread (or the piece of pitta bread). (Make sure that the loaf is the right size so you will be able to share it with everyone with no leftovers.) Explain that there are many slices in the bread but it is still one loaf — just as there are many people at Mass in the church, but we are all parts of one Body of Christ.

We eat from the one loaf to show that we are all together, we are in unity with one another. We also drink from the same cup to show that we are one family. When everyone has eaten and drunk the bread and the juice, invite them to go into the church.

Some advice for the session

Once again, keep this session simple:

- Move from your meeting place and gather outside the church and ask people to welcome one another as they do at a Sunday Mass.
- When they go into the church, invite those who are already baptised to bless themselves with holy water and tell them that, when they do this, they remind themselves of their baptism.
- Ask them to genuflect if they are able (and remind them of the reason for this action).
- Ask the priest to come into the church and go to the altar. Have a dish with unconsecrated hosts on it and a chalice with unconsecrated wine in it on the altar. Make sure people realise that this is not the "real thing". This bread and wine has not been blessed (or consecrated); it is not Jesus; this is a practice.
- The priest might read the Gospel from the altar, or he may go to the lectern. I suggest using the adapted version of St Paul's first letter to the Corinthians 11:23-25.

> On the night the Lord Jesus was betrayed,
> He took a loaf of bread. He gave thanks and broke it and said:
> "This is my body that is for you.
> Remember me when you do this."
> In the same way he took the cup after supper, and said:
> "This cup is the new covenant in my blood.
> Remember me when you drink it."

Giving the scripture message to each person

- If you can arrange people to be seated in such a way that it would be possible for the leader or the priest to give this message to each person again by holding their hands and looking into their eyes, saying:

> "[Name], Jesus says to you today: Remember me when you eat this bread and drink this wine. It is me and I love you."

- Invite people to say the Lord's Prayer if they are able and to offer one another the sign of peace explaining again why we do this. We are now ready to practise receiving Holy Communion.
- Explain that when we walk up to the altar, we should join our hands in prayer. While

processing up to the altar, think about Jesus, who we will be receiving.

- When you reach the priest or extraordinary minister of Holy Communion, he or she will say "Body of Christ" and we respond "Amen". This means "yes" I agree, I believe this really is Jesus. We can choose between receiving communion on the hand or on the tongue. If you receive on the hand, hold your left hand under your right one (of the other way around if you are left-handed) making a throne for your king, Jesus. Your hands should be held up in front of your heart because Jesus is about to come into your heart. Our open hands speak of an abiding sense that the divine generosity is available and expected.
- You then take the host, put it in your mouth and swallow it.
- If you choose to receive the host on your tongue, you hold your head up and put your tongue out. After the host is put onto your tongue, you swallow the host.
- If you are receiving from the chalice, move to the priest or extraordinary minister of Holy Communion. When s/he says "the Blood of Christ" you reply "Amen". You take a sip from the chalice and return to your seat.
- After practising receiving communion, encourage people to spend time in quiet prayer anticipating what it will be like to receive Jesus in the Eucharist; thanking Jesus for giving himself to them. After a pause, you might sing a communion hymn, such as Sebastian Temple's "Take my hands and make them as your own", Christine McCann's "Gifts of bread and wine", or CJM's "Bread of Life" and "Taste and See".

drawing by Kim Blundeel © 2014

Getting the message

Remember to give people plenty of time to hear Jesus is speaking to them today — and give them time to quieten down after the music and movement. This will bring the session to a close nicely.

Sharing the message/celebrating

It is time to have refreshments, to share with one another what it is like to prepare together to receive Holy Communion. Ask what they are most looking forward to as they receive Holy Communion for the first time, or how this session has helped them if they are already receiving Holy Communion.

✓ **Remember, for this session, you'll need:**

✓ **To introduce the session:**
- A focal point for the first part of the session:
- A table with a white table cloth;
- A loaf of bread (or a piece of pitta bread);
- A goblet with some juice;
- Flowers and a candle.

✓ **Activity and special place:**
- To have organised the priest to be present and the church to be available;
- To have invited some of the parish musicians;
- To have unconsecrated hosts and wine;
- The holy book with the simplified reading placed inside, draped cloth, a candle.

✓ **Music:**
- Sebastian Temple's "Take my hands and make them as your own"; or
- Christine McCann's "Gifts of bread and wine";
- CJM's "Bread of Life" and "Taste and See".

Celebrating the Eucharist

Session aim To learn or be reminded how to approach and receive Holy Communion.

Preparing for the session

In this session, we will be helping people find a way to participate better in the Mass. I suggest that you think about what happens during the different parts of the Mass by way of preparing yourself for the session. If you were asked to plan a celebration Mass for some occasion, would you know the order of the Mass?

In the session, we will be using Widgit symbols, which we will put into an empty church following what the priest does during Mass with the cards. You will find a template for an empty church and the Widgit cards on the additional resources CD. I suggest you use the box top of a box of A4 paper. Put the image of the church on the bottom of the box so that the cards won't fall about. Invite a priest and someone to read and distribute communion (or people who will play their parts). As they go through the order of the Mass, the

Fr John Chandler, First Communion Mass June 2013 St Joseph and St Edmund's Parish, Southampton

Photo: Richard Ashworth

candidates will move the Widgit symbols that match what they are doing.

John 6:48-51. 55-56

[48] *I am the bread of life.*
[49] *Your ancestors ate the manna in the wilderness and they died.*
[50] *This is the bread that comes down from heaven,*
  So that one may eat of it and not die.
[51] *I am the living bread that came down from heaven;*
  and this bread will live forever.
  Whoever eats of this bread will live forever
  and the bread that I will give for the life of the world is my flesh
[55] *For my flesh is true food and my blood is true drink.*
[56] *Those who eat my flesh and drink my blood*
  abide in me and I in them.

It would seem that this text, written possibly around AD 90, is a clear indication that the early Christian community believed Christ to be present in the bread and wine at their ritual meal. It was a simple celebration, with the "breaking of the bread" taking place during the meal. The importance of this fact cannot be overlooked. The early Christians continued to meet after the death and resurrection of Jesus.

At the Last Supper, Jesus said: "Do this in memory of me." His followers believed he was present in the bread and wine used at the fellowship meal. The great emphasis on the unity of the meal would seem to suggest that fellowship of those around the table was a strong theme of Eucharist in the early Church. The notion of a fellowship meal is an important religious theme; sharing a meal increases the unity among those present.

By way of preparing yourself for the session reflect on this idea of closeness with those we eat with. We don't invite people we don't like, people we don't want to be friends with, for a meal. Reflect on how eating with friends often brings you closer to them. Ask yourself how open you are to being true companions with your fellow parishioners. Make connections!

Note:

The word companion comes from the Latin: *com* meaning with and *panis* meaning bread. A companion is someone we break bread with, someone we sit down for a meal with.

Some advice for this session

The aim of this session is to find ways to help people understand and participate in the Mass The following pages describe what happens in the Mass. You will find symbol supported materials on the Mass prepared as an A6 booklet by St Joseph's Pastoral Centre. It is called Understanding the Mass and can be found on the St Joseph's website. You will also find an A5 booklet of an Anglican service called Holy Communion (written by Bishop John Davies), on the Widgit website. Both booklets can be printed free of charge. You may decide to use one of those booklets as the basis of your activity instead of (or in support of) what I suggest here.

Keep this activity simple:

Gather outside the church and welcome everyone as usual by name. Ask someone to offer people a copy of the next two pages or a set of Widgit cards. When they go into the church, invite people to bless themselves and to genuflect (and explain why we do this).

- Explain that, at Mass, we do what Jesus did in his life and, that, in this session we will see that. We will also have a template of the inside of a church and Widgit symbols that we can use to go through the order of the Mass. The additional resources CD has additional Widgit symbols that you can either add in (such as the penitential rite, the collection, and so on.) while you go through the comparison of Jesus' life to the order of the Mass. Alternatively, you can encourage people to take the set of cards and the template of the church with them when they come to Mass to help them follow the Mass.
- When the priest comes into the church and onto the sanctuary, ask people to move their Widgit priest to the same place and stop to explain that the first thing he will do is to greet people.

We talk about the five steps in the life of Christ:

"Come follow me" (Mark 1:18)

One of the first things Jesus did early on in his public life was to call some people to follow him. In this way, he formed a community; it is as members of a community of people that Christians come to God through Jesus.

"Listen to me, all of you, and understand" (Mark 7:15)

Once he had assembled his group, Jesus began to teach them the secret of his life. It was the story of his relationship with God, whom he called Father. The good news for his followers was that they were also now part of that relationship. This good news is also ours because of our baptism.

"Thanks he gave to God" (Matthew 14:19)

The followers of Jesus noticed that he prayed a good deal. His prayer was often one of giving thanks. Whenever he took and broke bread, he gave thanks. He often praised and thanked God his Father for the great things he was doing. Jesus was a thanking person.

"Take and eat. This is my body." (Matthew 26:26)

For a long time, Jesus wished to have this special meal with his disciples. It was at the Last Supper that he asked them to continue this action down through the ages in his memory: in memory of his life and in memory of his message. For twenty centuries now, Christians have remained true to this wish.

"Go out to the whole world, tell them the Good News and baptise them" (Mark 16:15 and Matthew 28:19)

This was the last command of Jesus before he ascended to his Father. Every time a Christian parent brings a child for baptism or tells them a story about Jesus, or leads the family in prayer, they are putting this into practice and inheriting a mighty blessing.

We talk about how the Mass mirrors those five steps

We come together

In the first part of the Mass, we become a community. People come together, believing that where two are three are gathered, Jesus is really present. People forgive one another and ask God to forgive them for the times when they have not been as loving as God wants them to be.

We listen

Catholics believe that when the scriptures are read in the Church, Jesus our Risen Lord himself, is present speaking to us just as when he walked the roads of Galilee. We, in turn, respond to him, and think about how this applies in our lives.

We give thanks

The central action of the Mass is that of giving thanks. The one who is being thanked is God the Father. He is being thanked for sending his Son, Jesus, as our Saviour. At Mass we remember that Jesus has died for us and that he was raised to life by the Father.

We take and eat

Through the action of the Holy Spirit, the bread and wine are changed into the Body and Blood of Christ. At communion, the people are joined more to Christ and are nourished by him, becoming more and more the Body of Christ.

We go out into the world to tell them the Good News

At the end of the Mass, the priest sends us out saying: "Go and announce the Gospel of the Lord" or "Go in peace, glorifying the Lord by your life" or "Go forth, the Mass is ended" or "Go in peace". We are sent out by Jesus himself, to live in such a way as to make the world a better place for others, especially the needy, as Jesus taught his followers to see him in the poor.

Leading the session

This depends on the ability of the people you are working with. If you are going to take people through the order of the Mass using the Widgit cards, ensure every participant has a full set of the cards and the template of the church from the additional resources CD. We've tried to include the main actions that take place during the Mass in the hopes that they will use them when they come to Mass to follow what is happening, and to help them engage in the Mass. If you feel your participants would benefit from having more cards, you can access the symbols through the Widgit and St Joseph's websites given in the Appendix. As always, you must personalise these materials and these activities to suit the needs of the people you are working with.

Getting the message

The group can then be invited to sit and say a "thank you" prayer to Jesus for inviting them to his house and for talking to them.

Finish the session with a lively "sending forth" hymn, for example: "We are walking in the light of God":

> We are marching in the light of God × 4
> We are marching, marching, we are marching — Oooo
> We are marching in the light of God

Verse 2: Same as one but replace light of God with "love of God"

Verse 3: Same again but with "moving in the power of God"

If possible, get a drummer and offer people percussion instruments and encourage them to dance from the church to the place where you will celebrate.

Sharing the message

It is time to celebrate, to share the Good News with one another. It is time to have refreshments, and share with one another the experiences of following this programme. Have they made new friends? Do they feel more at home in their parish community? Has it changed their understanding of the Mass? Are they looking forward to coming to Mass on Sunday, to using the booklet or Widgit puzzle? Are they looking forward to telling their friends and family what they have learned?

Most importantly, have they gained a sense that they are a Eucharistic people, a people who have a relationship with the living Christ? Have they become people who will bring Jesus into the world by the love they share with one another and by the care they offer to those in need?

 Remember, for this session, you'll need:

To introduce the session:
Talk about the kind of people we invite to have a meal with us.
They are normally friends, companions. Ask people to think about the people they meet at Mass.

Activity and special place:
You will need to invite the priest to join your session; a welcomer, a collector, an extraordinary minister of Holy Communion. You will need a catechist, a friend or a parent for each participant, to guide them through this exercise so that they will know how to follow it. You will also need to explain the exercise to whoever comes to Mass with them so that they will be able to help them. You will need an A6 or an A5 booklet for each participant, or a set of Widgit cards and a box with the image of an empty church.

Music both of which are available on YouTube:
• "I am the bread of life" by Suzanne Toolan, RSM.
• "We are marching in the light of God" Traditional South African, verse one translated by Anders Nyberg; verses two and three by Andrew Maries.
• "Bread of life, truth eternal" by CJM.

Christian prayer

True prayer brings us out of ourselves: it opens us to the Father and to the neediest of our brothers and sisters. This was a central part of Pope Francis' message to the faithful gathered for Mass on Saturday morning, 11 May 2013, in the chapel of the Domus Sancta Martha residence at the Vatican.

The Pope's homily focused on the day's Gospel reading, in which Jesus says: "If you ask the Father anything in my name, he will give it you."

Prayer can be boring, the Pope said, if it focuses on us; but true prayer is the turning out of ourselves and to the Father in the name of Jesus: true prayer is an exodus from ourselves. If we are not able to move out of ourselves and towards our brothers and sisters in need, to the sick, the ignorant, the poor, the exploited; if we are not able to accomplish this exodus from ourselves, and towards their wounds; we shall never learn that freedom, which carries us through that other exodus from ourselves, and towards the wounds of Jesus. There are two exits from ourselves: one to the wounds of Jesus, the other to the wounds of our brothers and sisters. This is what Jesus wants there to be in our prayer.

I hope you will find these materials prayerful and that they will help people with learning disabilities to enter into prayerful conversation with God, through Jesus in the Spirit.

I hope that the materials will encourage those who use them to move out of themselves towards our brothers and sisters in need, to recognise the gifts God has given to us and to identify ways they can use them for the good of others. In this way, I hope they will come to be aware of God's presence in their lives, in the world around them and in the people they meet.

We have not included traditional Catholic prayers in the sessions; we have focused more on creating a prayerful atmosphere, reflective prayer based on scripture and prayerful music. This doesn't mean that traditional prayers should not be included wherever possible. It is most important for all of us, especially people with learning disabilities, to know our traditional Catholic prayers so that we can join in with our parish communities at Mass. The following prayers can be downloaded free from the Widgit website (http://www.widgit.com/resources/curriculum/re/prayer_books/index.htm).
Each of them can be printed off as A5 booklets:

> The Sign of the Cross
> The Hail Mary
> The Lord's Prayer
> The Glory Be and
> The Angel of God

Diana Klein
January 2015

Photo: Diana Klein

Appendix: Resource Pack

to enable participation of people with learning disabilities in this programme

These materials can be used in a variety of ways and are particularly useful for children with autistic spectrum disorders and communication difficulties but have also been used and enjoyed by people of all ages and abilities to help discover, remember and share the Good News. For example, symbols can be used to enable the participants to respond in a meaningful way, to express their opinion, for example, about the session.

> Was the session good? Was it very good? Or, was it the best?

The cards in the pack can also be used when choices are to be made about which activity they like the most, which one they want to repeat.

Do they like arts and crafts, for example?
Is it chatting with their new friends that they like the best?

When it comes to scripture, to the religious dimension of the sessions,
do they like dressing up and acting out the Gospel?
What is it about coming to the sessions they like the best?
Is it the feeling of being welcome? Or, is it meeting new friends?
Or, is it taking care of each other?

For those who rely on symbols to communicate, the pack includes "yes" and "no" cards to help them answer questions posed to them.

This resource has been designed as a mediated learning experience tool. It is intended to provide enjoyable and anxiety free opportunities to mediate to people the events, people, meanings and messages of the Good News and relate them to their lives today. Although, this resource has been used throughout this book to encourage responses, you may want to access the whole pack so that you can make the most of these opportunities, particularly for people who are non-verbal. You will find it on the St Joseph's website (www.stjoseph.org.uk).

Was the session

 good?

 very good?

 the best?

arts and crafts

chatting with friends

acting out the Gospel

feeling welcome

meeting new friends

taking care of each other

yes   no

Reference materials, Church teaching and State documents

Essential resources

St Joseph's Pastoral Centre provides resources on its website (http://www.stjoseph.org.uk/):

- Pack to enable participation of people with learning disabilities in this resource is available on the website free of charge. It contains templates for Widgit cards to help engage people in responding and sharing with one another. The cards have been used throughout the materials as part of the sessions; but for a full explanation of the resource, see p. 187.
- You can print the A6 symbol supported booklets for the Mass, which can be printed for each participant free of charge.
- Activity materials will be added as they are available. Some of them may demand a small fee.

Widgit provides resources on their website (http://www.widgit.com/resources/curriculum/re/prayer_ books/index.htm):

- Free resources: You will find a free resource of a symbol supported Holy Communion service using Widgit symbols. The complete service can be printed out in an A5 booklet.
- A full range of materials and images are available from Widget for a small fee. If you are using their images, you should be contributing to the cost of their work.

I Call You Friends resources are available on the Widgit website (http://www.widgit.com/resources/curriculum/re/i_call_you_friends/index.htm) for a small fee.

ADHD and ADD: www.nhs.uk/condiitons/attention-deficit-hyperactivity-disorder; www.chadd.org; www.add.org; www.help4add.org

Asperger syndrome: www.sense.org.uk

Reference materials

The Catechism of the Catholic Church, Geoffrey Chapman, London, 1994

Catechesi Tradendae (On Catechesis in our Time), Pope John Paul II, 1979

Children and Families Bill 2013 is before Parliament at the time of writing (which includes clauses which reform the system of support for children with special educational needs).

Code of Canon Law, Libreria Editrice Vaticana (available on line: http://www.vatican.va/archive/ENG1104/_INDEX.HTM)

Disability movement- '*Who says, who controls*' The Chronically Sick and Disabled Persons Act (CSDP), 1970 — the duty to consider needs of disabled persons

Equality Act: The Equality Act 2010 aims to protect disabled people and prevent disability discrimination. It provides legal rights for disabled people in the areas of: employment, education, access to goods, services and facilities, buying and renting land or property, functions of public bodies, for example the issuing of licences.

The General Directory for Catechesis (GDC) 189; Congregation for the Clergy, Catholic Truth Society, London, 1997

Human Rights Act, 1998 aims to give further effect to rights and freedoms guaranteed under the European Convention on Human Rights

Pastoral Statement of the US Catholic Bishops on Persons with Disabilities, 1998

The Person with Disabilities: the duties of the civil and ecclesial community. Vatican, 2000 is the Catholic Church's version of the 1998 statement issued by the United Nations Human Rights Commission.

The Rite of Christian Initiation of Adults (RCIA); The Office of the Sacred Congregation for Divine Worship, 1988

Welcome and Justice for Persons with Disabilities, a framework of access and inclusion, a statement of the US Bishops, 1999

Valuing Difference: People with disabilities in the life and mission of the Church, Bishops' Conference of England and Wales, 1998

Valuing people: a new strategy for learning disability for the 21st century, 2001, is the first White Paper on learning disability for thirty years and sets out an ambitious and challenging programme of action for improving services.

Index

Photo credits:

Photo Art

Focal points

Illustrations and drawings

Published by Redemptorist Publications
Alphonsus House, Chawton, Hampshire, GU34 3HQ, UK
Tel. +44 (0)1420 88222, Fax. +44 (0)1420 88805
Email rp@rpbooks.co.uk, www.rpbooks.co.uk

A registered charity limited by guarantee
Registered in England 3261721

Text by Diana Klein in collaboration with St Joseph's Pastoral Centre
Edited by Yvonne Fordyce
Designer: Diana Klein

ISBN 978-0-85231-425-8

A CIP catalogue record for this book is available from the British Library.

St Joseph's Pastoral Centre is grateful to the National Council of the Churches of Christ in the USA for the use of the New Revised Standard Version Bible: Catholic Edition copyright ©1993 and 1989. All rights reserved.

Printed by Lithgo Press Ltd, Leicester LE8 6NU